GATHERED
for GOOD

JONATHAN
GRIFFITHS

GATHERED
for GOOD

GOD'S GOOD DESIGN FOR
the LOCAL CHURCH

B&H
PUBLISHING®
BRENTWOOD, TENNESSEE

978-1-4300-9632-0

Published by B&H Publishing Group
Brentwood, Tennessee

Dewey Decimal Classification: 262.7
Subject Heading: CHURCH / CHURCH FELLOWSHIP /
CHURCH MEMBERSHIP

Cover design by Gearbox. Images by Artishok and sathaporn/
Shutterstock. Author photo by COUVRETTE/OTTAWA.

1 2 3 4 5 6 • 28 27 26 25

To the saints of The Metropolitan Bible Church—
gathered for much good

Acknowledgments

THIS BOOK HAS TAKEN SHAPE WITHIN THE LIFE OF A REAL and vibrant church family. I am so grateful for the fellowship and stimulus of brothers and sisters in Christ at The Met, who together strive to live out the biblical principles set out in this book. It has been a joy to teach these truths to a congregation that desires to grow more and more into the kind of church that honours and pleases the Saviour. As ever, I am thankful for the encouragement of our elders to view writing as part of my ministry and service to the wider family of God.

My personal editor, Danielle DuRant, has helped me sharpen and clarify so much of this material, and I am in her debt for her careful and judicious work on the manuscript.

It has been a privilege to work with Logan Pyron and the excellent team at B&H, and I value greatly the opportunity to partner with them in this project.

As always, my ability to create space for writing in the midst of life and ministry rests on the good graces and patience of my wife, Gemma, and our three children. I am more thankful to them and for them than I can adequately express.

Contents

Foreword

FOR YEARS I HAVE LAID CLAIM TO THE TITLE OF "GOD'S spoiled child." I genuinely consider myself the most blessed man alive. With full awareness that God loves all His children perfectly, I nonetheless feel that I have lived a life brimming with more blessings and overflowing with greater favor than any of my contemporaries. Others may certainly have more money, but no one has greater wealth. Undoubtedly many have more possessions, but no one could have a greater treasure of people than those God has placed in my life. From my childhood to today, the matrix of faithful family, heartwarming friendships, and rich relationships constantly testifies of God's benevolence.

Most of those relationships have a common source: the church. Not only was I born and reared in a Christian home, but in a *pastor's* home. My father was my mentor, evangelist, discipler, best friend, and example. His warm and joyful spirit helped me to love the church and the people of God—which was a great grace, because we went to church *all the time*! We attended services on Sunday mornings, Sunday nights, Wednesday nights, monthly youth fellowship meetings, revival meetings, Vacation Bible School, and Bible conferences—*lots* of Bible conferences. Nearly all holidays were spent at a church holding a conference where I would hear (mostly) good preaching and hang out with other preachers' kids, many of whom have remained lifelong friends.

Though I don't assume everyone should attend church as frequently as we did, I count it as one of God's greatest blessings in my life. I have had a front row seat to closely observe God's gracious work in thousands of lives, marriages, and homes. I have seen brokenness, waywardness, sinfulness, and a lot of quirkiness, but I have also witnessed repentance, redemption, restoration, and deep relationships. I have watched the bonds of mutual mercy and grace weave disparate lives together like nothing else on earth can. All those years I thought we were just going to church, but we were really joining with our brothers and sisters to hear our Father tell us all how much He loved us and how wonderfully we fit in His family, how much we *belong*.

Every heart yearns to belong. We look for our group. We connect with our cluster. We hunt in packs. Even misfits find each other and hang out together. We seek solace or sustenance or reassurance in assembling ourselves together.

People who love the same thing find themselves inexorably drawn to each other. We search for others who share the same devotion we feel for whatever passion we pursue: our preferred sport, favorite team, chosen career, or dream car. Upon discovering others who love what we love, we organize ourselves into fan clubs, alumni chapters, career guilds, service organizations, or some other league that expresses and affirms our mutual affection. The deeper the love, the greater the gravitational attraction pulling us into the same orbit. Doesn't it make sense that the saving love of Christ, the greatest love the world has ever known, would result in the strongest bonds the world has ever experienced?

We desire fellowship, companionship, and love, not primarily because we are deficient or needy—though we may be—but because we are created in the image of God. Affection, fellowship, and love, after all, are at the very center of the Godhead. Father, Son, and Holy Spirit share perfect love and maintain perfect fellowship and perfect unity.

Salvation makes it possible for us—fallen, broken, and sinful, but redeemed—to enter into the life, love, and glory that existed in the Triune God before the world was formed. Though God sets His love on us as individuals, His love draws us also to others whom He loves. The very nature of God and of His love makes us seek to express that love as He does—in loving fellowship and unity in the character and will of God.

To put it quite simply and starkly, we cannot fulfill the commands of the New Testament by ourselves, nor can we express the character of the love that God has shed abroad in our hearts by living a solitary, ascetic, monkish kind of Christianity. Jesus chose twelve "that they might be *with* Him" (Mark 3:14, emphasis added). He prayed that "the love with which you have loved me may be in them, and I in them" (John 17:26, emphasis added). He taught that the worst thing that could happen to one of his disciples was not death, but *solitude.* "Truly, truly, I say to you, unless a grain of wheat falls into the earth and dies, it remains *alone*; but if it dies, it bears much fruit" (John 12:24). Most important, He established His church—His *assembly*—so that we might be together. No honest reading of the New Testament can justify a Christian life without regularly gathering with other Christians for worship, prayer, encouragement, teaching, and sharing life together.

Reading *Gathered for Good* stirred my heart and warmed my soul more than any book I have read recently. Jonathan Griffiths writes like a father inviting his large, extended family to a beautiful banquet, whetting our appetites by telling us just how good it will feel to be together. The food will be sumptuous and plentiful. The fellowship will be encouraging and joyful. Our tired hearts will be reminded just how blessed we are to have each other and to go through life together.

The challenge of maintaining meaningful connections has never been greater. Our age is characterized by technological advancements and societal shifts that roil our lives, yet the call to gather remains ever relevant and even more deeply necessary. *Gathered for God* serves as both a reminder and a guide, urging us to embrace the biblical mandate of community, encouraging us to move beyond virtual interactions and seek the richness of face-to-face and heart-to-heart fellowship, where love, accountability, and spiritual growth flourish.

I'm sure I am not the only one of God's children who feels like I have enjoyed more of my heavenly Father's blessings than anyone else. I suspect many other believers, cognizant of God's daily mercies and eternal love, feel especially favored. But I am equally convinced that this awareness of the depth of God's love and the goodness of God's grace is inextricably linked to the frequent experience of those things in the gathered church. That is where the matrix of faithful family, heartwarming friendships, and rich relationships constantly testifies of God's benevolence. Who would not want that?

Hershel York
Dean of The School of Theology and the Victor and
Louise Lester Professor of Christian Preaching

. . . .

God's Good Design
for Gathering

THERE IS A STRONG TEMPTATION TO GO IT ALONE IN THE
Christian life, to try Christianity without church. After all,
church is costly. People are complicated, and many of us have
had experiences with churches that have been painful and
heartbreaking. Added to those negative factors, the draw of
remote and privatized faith has increased with technology. We
can access fabulous resources for learning and growing from all
over the world. We can enjoy "worship experiences" of various
kinds from the comfort of our home. Many of us have been
forced to experience aspects of church life remotely during the

time of the coronavirus pandemic. For some, this has been a welcome change, and going back to church holds questionable appeal.

But let me ask you: Have you been less involved in church life lately? If you have never really committed yourself to a local church, how has it been going for you? How have you found walking alone and flying solo in the Christian life? How is your spiritual health? How is your mental health? Do you feel surrounded by other believers or supported in your Christian walk? How is your battle with sin? How is your walk with the Savior? How is your growth in knowledge of the Word? Are you holding lightly to the things of this world and prizing the things of God's kingdom?

I ask these questions because, as a pastor who has the privilege of interacting with many believers, I have found that our spiritual vitality is tied closely to our involvement and investment in a healthy local church. If we do not value, prioritize, and invest in church, we cannot walk in strength and grow in maturity in the Christian life.

It may well be that you are struggling in your own spiritual life. You may feel dry, isolated, trapped in sin, or even despondent. You have been caught in a bad place, and you have felt stuck for a long time. You are aware of the symptoms of joylessness, loneliness, discouragement, or despair, but you have not been able to pin down the cause. Now, I can hardly pretend to know you and your situation, but in light of experience, I would want to ask, "What is the nature of your involvement in the life of a vibrant Christian community?" The correlation between our spiritual health and our church involvement is often much closer than we may think.

Further questions require our attention and careful reflection in light of Scripture. How far can I go it alone in following Jesus? What is the place of Christian community in my own discipleship? What is a healthy model for the local church, and what are the key elements of the biblical mandate for church life? If I am to participate in church for my good and for the good of others, what should this look like? What should I expect to give and to receive?

This short book is an invitation to look afresh at the goodness, necessity, and value of Christian community within the local church. After a season of unprecedented disruption to global church life by the coronavirus pandemic, we have the privilege of an opportunity to make a fresh start in church life according to healthy patterns and biblical principles. Above all, I hope to encourage you to invest deeply in the life of the local church for your own benefit, for the encouragement of others, and ultimately, for the glory of God.

The conviction underlying this book is that God speaks to us through His Word. If God has made His will for us known to us in His Word, then we can only expect to flourish and grow as His people through listening and responding in repentance, faith, and obedience. We will attempt to trace out some key themes and emphases from the Bible relating to the community life of the people of God.

As we do so, I believe we will see together that church is not an optional extra for the Christian, but rather lies at the heart of the saving purpose of God. You may know that the words *church* and *congregation* are English translations of the Greek word *ekklēsia*, which means "gathering." The church is the "gathering" of God's people. This idea of "gathering" is loaded with meaning in the Bible and takes us to the heart of the gospel.

In the beginning, when God made Adam and Eve, these two first humans lived in the presence of God, in His place of sanctuary and blessing within the garden of Eden. When they rebelled against Him, they were sent out of His presence into the wider world with all its uncertainties. This was the first "scattering" of humanity. As the human family grew, they sought to gather together to build a great tower to the heavens, even to ascend to the place of God (Gen. 11). But God scrambled their language and scattered them once more in another act of judgment.

At this point, it may appear that God was only in the business of *scattering* sinners. But God's plan was not only to scatter in judgment but also to gather in grace. He called the people of Israel to Himself and brought them out of bondage in Egypt to the wilderness, where they were His own "congregation" en route to the promised land. They, too, experienced scattering in judgment, not least through the Assyrian assault and the loss of the ten northern tribes. Nonetheless, God still engaged in gathering people—and not just from one nation but from all the nations of the world.

Ultimately, God demonstrated His remarkable grace in Jesus, who called all people to repent, believe the gospel, and follow Him. Jesus promised that when He was lifted up on the cross, and then raised in His resurrection and ascension, He would gather all people to Himself (John 12:32). And that is what He did. He gathered people from every tribe, tongue, and nation, and He is still gathering. He broke down the barrier between God and us and between each of us. His church is the demonstration and manifestation of His saving plan to draw together a people scattered by sin into wholesome, life-giving community.

God has called us together to something profoundly good: gathering shaped by grace that nourishes God's people in grace and extends the message of grace to a needy world. *Gathered for Good* invites us to invest deeply in the work of God and the people of God because Christ's grace has captivated and transformed us. Our project now is to see how that is meant to work and how we can invest, for our good and God's glory, in the life of the local church.

1

· · · · · · ·

Gathered to
One Another

IN THE GLORY DAYS OF THE AGE OF SAILING, SHIPS WOULD fly their national colors on their mast as they entered battle. If a ship ever lowered its flag—lowered its "colors"—it was a sign of distress or even surrender.

In October 1797, British and Dutch ships met off the coast of Holland at the Battle of Camperdown. The fighting was fierce and, in the middle of the skirmish, the British ship *HMS Venerable* was damaged and its main mast was broken. It was a disaster. The *Venerable* carried the Union flag, the command flag of the admiral of the fleet. Things looked bad, to say the least. If the British thought their admiral was sinking, the battle was almost certainly lost. But rather than accept defeat, a low-ranking crew member named Jack Crawford climbed what was left of the mast. Under heavy fire from Dutch canons, he nailed the colors to the splinters of the mast. Buoyed by his courage, the British went on to win the battle and capture eleven Dutch ships without a loss to their fleet.

The Battle of Camperdown is the substance of nautical history and, indeed, legend. Ever since, the phrase "nail your colors to the mast" has meant to pledge your undying loyalty to your people, to commit to standing firm to the end.

Scripture calls us to unwavering devotion to one another. As we consider what kind of community God calls us to be, my prayer is that you will be moved to nail your colors to the mast and, out of love for Jesus, affirm your devotion to His church. If you are committed to a local fellowship of believers, I encourage you to go deeper into that commitment. If you are on the periphery of church life, I want to invite you to move to the core.

For those of you who are part of a large church, I particularly want to speak to you at the outset of this chapter. Attending a large church can be a wonderful blessing with many ministry opportunities and mission and outreach initiatives. Nevertheless, this privilege can bring dangers. Perhaps chief among them is that it is easy to stay on the margins, to be only nominally involved, to slide in and out on Sundays without being noticed or becoming engaged. In a smaller fellowship, that is harder to do. For some readers, that dynamic may well be the reason you started attending your church in the first place. Maybe you needed a lower profile for a season. That can be understandable. However, when marginal Christian living becomes your pattern and a part of your church culture, it soon becomes a problem.

This chapter addresses commitment and gathering to one another. We instinctively commit to people we care for; we want to be in their lives instead of on the margins. Even so, commitment can be difficult to read about and even more difficult to put into action. I want to encourage you to nail your colors to the mast and to devote yourself to your local church community in the way the Bible teaches: gathered to one another.

What follows is a broad vision for Christian life, or *four reasons why you should nail your colors to the mast.*

One, you need to care for others. Caring for others is a central New Testament theme. In his letter to the Romans, the apostle Paul explains how the gospel will impact and transform their lives. In chapter 12, he makes an impassioned call for the Roman church to give themselves as living sacrifices in response to God's mercy. He calls on them to use their gifts to serve the body of Christ, and then he writes:

Let love be genuine. Abhor what is evil; hold
fast to what is good. Love one another with
brotherly affection. Outdo one another in
showing honor. Do not be slothful in zeal, be
fervent in spirit, serve the Lord. Rejoice in
hope, be patient in tribulation, be constant in
prayer. Contribute to the needs of the saints
and seek to show hospitality. (Rom. 12:9–13)

You and I can easily think of our faith in individualistic
terms. My spiritual life is about *my* sins being forgiven, *my* walk
with Jesus, *my* hope for the future, *my* needs, *my* growth. Yet the
whole sweep of God's salvation plan demonstrates His interest in not only saving individuals but also creating a wholly
new people and a wholly new society. God gathers us to one
another for our good and for His glory. We need others to care
for us, and we need to care for one another. In this new society,
God says we will interact with one another in ways that might
seem strange to the watching world. Scripture calls each of us
to honor our brothers and sisters above ourselves and to share
with those who are in need (Rom. 12:10, 13). The local church
is to be the place, in the midst of a lonely world, where there
is true and rich community. It is to be the place, in a heartless
and insensitive world, where there is abundant care. It is to be
the place, in a greedy world, where there is abundant generosity.

In short, the church is to be a new kind of society where love, as Paul makes clear, is genuine and deep; where evil is abhorred, but good is treasured and practiced (v. 9). It is where brotherly and sisterly affection mark relationships, where people are tripping over one another to outdo one another in showing honor in the way they speak to and about one another (v. 10). The church is where people are serving together zealously (v. 11); where they are rejoicing together in the hope of the gospel and waiting patiently through difficulties, praying together in all things (v. 12). It is to be a place where those who have resources are contributing to the needs of other believers so that God's people will not be in need. It is a place where homes are open and hospitality is the norm (v. 13).

Paul's picture is a wonderful vision of Christ-centered living. And it is thrilling and joyful to see this biblical vision lived out—as I have seen personally in a number of churches where I have had the privilege of ministry involvement and leadership. People step in to help financially when others face challenging times; the sick are visited and cared for; meals are made for those going through a difficult season; homes are furnished for the young who are starting out. These are wonderful things to see. Nonetheless, such care only happens when the church is together and engaged in one another's lives. Such commitment only happens when you nail your colors to the mast and say:

This is my church. This is my family. These are my people. This is my spiritual home.

Have you done that in your own church? If not, will you? God's design for your Christian life is that you belong to a community and commit to others in this way. If you are someone who comes and goes quietly and is not really a part of the life of the church, let me gently say to you: "You are missing out, and your church is missing out too." We need to care for one another. This is just one reason to devote ourselves to one another in the local church.

Two, you need to minister to others. How easily we imagine church as a spiritual vending machine, as a place to go as a consumer to receive ministry. The design of many church buildings can compound this impression. Often, in many modern church buildings (at least in North America), if we squint our eyes a little and blur our vision, we can imagine that we are sitting in a movie theater with a platform at the front and comfortable seats in rows. We may feel more like spectators than participants.

In fact, I had a conversation recently with someone who asked me which church I worked for—she knew I was a pastor somewhere, but did not know where. I told her it was The Metropolitan Bible Church in Ottawa.

She responded by saying, "Oh yes, that is the one that used to be down on Bank Street, in an old movie theater." She was *almost* right, but not quite.

I said, "Well, yes, the church was on Bank Street, but the building was never a movie theater. It just looked a little like one."

(The façade of the old building still does look like a movie theater.)

I continued, "When the church was built at the end of the Great Depression, the bank would only risk financing the construction if it was built in such a way that it could easily be converted into a movie theater if the venture failed." It was wonderful that the church secured the financing to build, but the visual association was a little unfortunate!

How easily we can come to church as spectators. Sometimes all that is lacking is popcorn, we might think.

Of course, that was never God's design or intention. The New Testament teaches us that the church is to be a community where all the members are active in ministering the Word of God to one another. In fact, Paul writes in his letter to the Ephesians that the risen Lord Jesus gave specially called people as gifts to His church:

> And he gave the apostles, the prophets, the evangelists, the shepherds and teachers, to equip the saints for the work of ministry, for building

up the body of Christ, until we all attain to the unity of the faith and of the knowledge of the Son of God, to mature manhood, to the measure of the stature of the fullness of Christ, so that we may no longer be children, tossed to and fro by the waves and carried about by every wind of doctrine, by human cunning, by craftiness in deceitful schemes. Rather, speaking the truth in love, we are to grow up in every way into him who is the head, into Christ, from whom the whole body, joined and held together by every joint with which it is equipped, when each part is working properly, makes the body grow so that it builds itself up in love. (Eph. 4:11–16)

The risen Jesus gave particular people to the church (v. 11). These people included shepherds (or "pastors"; it is the same word in the original Greek) and teachers. These two terms probably refer together to just one kind of person: "the pastor-teacher." Now, we might assume, given the way in which many churches seem to function, Paul would go on in verse 12 to say something like: *The pastor-teacher is given to the church to do all the ministry so that the saints can be blessed when they come to church on Sunday morning.* But he does not. What does he say? The risen Jesus gave these leaders in order "to equip the saints for the work of ministry." That is, the saints are to *be equipped* for the heavy lifting together. The saints are to minister to one another. And that is why we must close the popcorn kiosk; Paul is telling us that we go to church not to take in a show but to engage in ministry. The pastor-teacher's role of spoken word ministry is important, yes, but its main goal is to equip the rest of the church for the ministry they are going to do: ministry from one another and to one another.

In other words, Paul indicates that pastor-teachers are not the frontline players—which is good, because I think I would survive about half of a second in a serious football game! No, pastor-teachers are more like coaches. Their job is to help the whole church family get on the field and do the hard work of ministry.

The saints do the work of ministry to build up the body (v. 12), so that everyone might grow in unity of the faith and in the knowledge of the Son of God (v. 13). Growing saints are no longer children in doctrinal terms, tossed around by every new idea that comes along (v. 14). Rather, each member of the body speaks the truth of God's Word in love so that all grow in Christ (v. 15). Each does his or her part to help the whole grow (v. 16). What a beautiful picture. What a wonderful design God has for the church!

For many churches, the ministry needs and opportunities that exist within its reach are huge. More often, their pastoral staff (however large or small) will be unable to meet them all.

But collectively, the church body will know a great deal of what is happening in the lives of its individuals and will often be able to meet those needs.

The collective ministry happens on Sunday, in the first place, when we gather with others to sing and declare words of truth to encourage one another in worship. The ministry continues after the service as members discuss what they have heard from Scripture and share words of gospel-shaped encouragement to one another in conversation. Ministry then continues throughout the week as church members meet formally or informally in Bible study groups, prayer meetings, and one another's homes.

Ministry is a team effort, and we are all involved. We need to minister to one another. That is what it means to be part of the body of Christ. But it will not happen if you are on the sidelines. Ministry will not happen if you are not known and if you do not know others. And so, here again, you need to nail your colors to the mast and declare yourself part of a church family.

Three, you need accountability. I was greatly encouraged recently while having coffee with a man who had visited our church many times over the last few years. The Lord has accomplished an amazing work in his life. He is barely recognizable from who he was. He had moved away to another part of the country but was in town and wanted to meet. I asked him if he had found a church home in his new community. He had, and he added that he looked for a church where he would be kept accountable for continuing to follow Jesus and live for Him. He did not want to be in a church where he could hide from others.

This was incredibly wise, but that desire does not come naturally. In fact, for this man, I think it only came because he knew practically and experientially how much he needed that accountability.

We could all go to church and hide if we wanted, but we all need accountability. We need to be where we can be challenged and helped if we are going off the rails in our walk with Jesus. Indeed, the Lord has given and established the local church as a safety net. Consider this verse:

> Obey your leaders and submit to them, for they are keeping watch over your souls, as those who will have to give an account. Let them do this with joy and not with groaning, for that would be of no advantage to you. (Heb. 13:17)

According to the writer to the Hebrews, the leaders of a local church have an incredibly significant responsibility: they watch over the souls of the church community. Moreover, they will have to give an account for their care to the chief Shepherd, Jesus. How sobering! Those aspiring to church leadership should think carefully before taking on that responsibility. But speaking from experience (and, here, I know I also speak for others), church leaders are not always certain of the identity of the souls that fall under their care. That is, a culture of marginality can obscure who is actually part of the church family and, thus, under the oversight of its leaders.

If you are part of a church and have held back from any formal commitment, then it will likely be difficult for the church leaders to navigate the situation. Godly leaders want to provide oversight, accountability, and spiritual protection for their church. If you have a fluid approach to church life, your church leader may not know where you stand. So let me encourage you: if you have not yet done so, commit yourself to a local church.

Churches in various times and places live out commitment in numerous ways. A formal membership of the kind that exists in the church I pastor is not the only way to do it, I am sure, but Hebrews 13:17 offers guidance. God calls you to commit to honor and follow your church leaders; in turn, the leaders commit to care for you. We all need this. If you are someone who lives on the margins of church life, I want to encourage you, in your local church setting and in the way that is appropriate there, to nail your colors to the mast. We need to be accountable to one another; accountability is essential to our Christian life.

Four, you need to stand with others. In the West, we have enjoyed two or three centuries of incredible favor as Christians. We have lived under remarkable freedom for a long time. Nevertheless, we must recognize significant changes that are taking place as well. We have floated a long way downstream from the Judeo-Christian headwaters in our culture and institutions throughout the West. I am sure you are probably well aware of this. You probably see and experience it every day, and you will have your own observations and perspectives, no doubt. The Lord has been gracious in sparing Christians in the West real persecution for a long time, even while believers in other parts of the world have faced terrible opposition. Maybe we will continue to enjoy freedom of religion for years to come here in North America where I live, but I do not think it is obvious that we will. We cannot assume it. Only the Lord knows the future.

Still, however things may develop and change over the coming years, we should prepare ourselves to be increasingly out of step with the culture. We should expect following Jesus to be more difficult and costly. As we prepare for whatever may come, therefore, we must seek to stand together as the people of God. When the pressure rises, the great temptation will be to run into the shadows. We need to commit ourselves to stand firm and to be unashamed of the gospel and of the church of Jesus Christ. The temptation to run when the heat rises is nothing new, of course. Jesus's disciples were tempted to run when He faced opposition, and, of course, they all deserted Him at the cross.

Peter's denial is perhaps the most famous desertion and denial in the Gospel accounts. His beautiful New Testament letters speak into a context of Christians enduring real persecution for their faith. Interestingly, Peter underscores the importance of Christians loving one another well through the difficulties they face. In his first letter, having addressed the reality of suffering and persecution for the faith, he writes:

> The end of all things is at hand; therefore be self-controlled and sober-minded for the sake of your prayers. Above all, keep loving one another earnestly, since love covers a multitude of sins. Show hospitality to one another without grumbling. As each has received a gift, use it to serve one another, as good stewards of God's varied grace. (1 Pet. 4:7–10)

Persecution may be on the horizon. But one day Jesus is going to return. In the meantime, and above all else, Peter says, keep on being the church. Keep on being faithful stewards of God's grace. Love one another. Show hospitality. Use your gifts to serve one another. Do not give up. Do not back away from the fellowship. Do not abandon one another. When the pressure mounts, stick together and continue being the body of Christ together.

We need to prepare ourselves for changing times. We need to anticipate a less comfortable future and ready our hearts and minds for pressure and even opposition. If you are already on the margins of church life, the temptation will be to slip away quietly when things become more challenging. But that must not happen. We are going to need one another more and more. We will need to stand together and publicly say we belong to Christ, we honor His Word, we are committed to His people, and we are part of His body.

Your local church community is at the heart of God's plans for the gospel and the world. So nail your colors to the mast. Devote yourselves to one another. And most importantly, gather and commit to others because you treasure Jesus more than anything else. If you love Christ, you love His people.

2

. . . .

Gathered to
Meet Together

WHAT WAS THE REASON YOU LAST ATTENDED CHURCH?

If you are a regular church attender or member, have you considered why you choose to gather with others week after week? Are these gatherings necessary for your Christian growth and witness? Could we not do things another way?

I believe if we have been captivated by God's grace, we will invest in His work and His people. Nonetheless, we still may struggle to answer the question: Why is it important to meet together? We might eventually come up with an answer related to worship: *We need to be here so we can worship God.*

Surely that is not a wrong answer; worship is at the heart of what we do when we gather. But if we search the Bible for the verse that says Christians meet together on Sunday morning for worship, we will not find that verse.

Even though we often tie the language of "worship" to our Sunday gatherings—and usually only in reference to *singing*—the New Testament rarely does that, if ever. The New Testament's picture of worship is much broader. Indeed, worship in the age of the new covenant, for redeemed and Spirit-filled people, is what we do with our whole lives. We are to live lives of worship to God wherever we are and in whatever we are doing.

Romans 12:1 encapsulates the New Testament's theology of worship. The apostle Paul writes: "I appeal to you therefore, brothers, by the mercies of God, to present your bodies as a living sacrifice, holy and acceptable to God, which is your spiritual worship." Paul then speaks of practical, week-round, 24–7 activities: using your gifts to serve the church, loving others well, practicing generosity and hospitality, and so on. We may imagine that a few minutes of hearty singing on a Sunday morning exhausts our worshipping responsibilities so that we are then off the hook to use the remaining 167 hours of the week as we choose. However, the Bible tells us that the whole of life is worship. Whether I am driving my car, doing my job, caring for my kids, interacting with my spouse, paying my taxes, or watching

TV, whatever I am doing is part of my worship. In everything, I am laying down my life on the altar for Jesus Christ.

Now, if all of life is worship, gathering in church on a Sunday morning should be worship too. Meeting together is a special expression of our worship, but it is definitely *not* the sum total of our worship.

So, what is significant about *corporate worship?* Why do we gather as the body of Christ on a Sunday morning? What aspects of Christian worship are unique as we meet corporately?

A full theology of corporate worship could span several chapters or even books. Scripture has much to say about worshipping together! Thus, what follows is only part of the picture.

We might consider corporate worship—and why it matters—in terms of our *eyes,* our *ears,* and our *mouths.* With those in mind, I want to suggest three reasons meeting together in worship matters immensely.

One, corporate worship opens our eyes to see God's grand design. Seeing the plans for a new building or development often generates excitement. What was once an idea now looks closer to a finished structure. Of course, the new software used by architects and designers can give you the sense that you are viewing actual photographs of a finished building instead of merely mock-ups.

Perhaps you have had the experience of buying a new home from a builder's plans. You can often go to the area where a new subdivision will be built and see a few model homes. You might encounter muddy fields, but the builders have put in a short section of road and built a few model homes to explore. When you walk through and look them over, you can visualize what is to come.

One of the remarkably interesting *big themes* of the Bible is the theme of scattering and gathering. I addressed this briefly in the introduction. The Bible shows us clearly that sin and judgment have the effect of scattering people from the presence of God and from one another. Even so, in redemption, God is at work gathering people together by gathering people to Himself first.

Think about Eden. God created two people, Adam and Eve, to enjoy His presence and each other's. God brought them into His presence for His glory and their good. Then they sinned, and what happened? They were sent out. They were expelled from the perfect bliss of Eden. Later in the human story, Scripture records further rebellion and the flood, yet God shows grace to Noah and his family in allowing humanity to continue (Gen. 6–8). But soon again, humans defy God by constructing the Tower of Babel to reach up to heaven and usurp His place. How does God respond in judgment? He scrambles their common language so they cannot collaborate against Him any longer, and then He scatters them from that place (Gen. 11).

Sin and judgment lead to scattering and alienation. But in redemption, God gathers people back into His presence. He begins by calling Abraham. He sets apart one family who will be His people and promises, through them, to bless the nations of the world.

The nation of Israel grows. God rescues them from slavery in Egypt and takes them toward the promised land He provides. He gathers them as a "congregation in the wilderness" (Deut. 31:30; Acts 7:38). They are a congregation and a gathering, which the New Testament will call "church." *Church* means "gathering," "assembly," "congregation."

Throughout the Old Testament, we witness periods when God gathers His people securely in their land and times of judgment when He scatters them.

Now let us zoom forward to the New Testament. When Jesus comes on the scene, He calls people to come to Him and follow Him. He gathers people together, and they are drawn to Him. Jesus then goes to the cross and dies for our sins, removing the barrier between God and His people. They can come back into His presence, even as Adam and Eve were in His presence in Eden. Moreover, this gospel of grace extends to both Jews and Gentiles. It gathers people from every nation.

The grand finale and ultimate plan are depicted in Revelation 7:

After this I looked, and behold, a great multitude that no one could number, from every nation, from all tribes and peoples and languages, standing before the throne and before the Lamb, clothed in white robes, with palm branches in their hands, and crying out with a loud voice, "Salvation belongs to our God who sits on the throne, and to the Lamb!" And all the angels were standing around the throne and around the elders and the four living creatures, and they fell on their faces before the throne and worshiped God, saying, "Amen! Blessing and glory and wisdom and thanksgiving and honor and power and might be to our God forever and ever! Amen." (vv. 9–12)

God's ultimate plan is for a redeemed people to gather in His presence around His throne to praise and worship Him for all eternity. We will gather from every nation, tribe, people, and language to be together because, at the cross, Jesus removed the barriers that separate us from one another and from our God.

Likewise, when we gather week by week as an "assembly" or "congregation"—to use language that goes back to Deuteronomy—in the presence of God to hear His Word and sing His praises, we experience a foretaste of our eternal destiny and home. We look around and see a glimpse of God's great plan and our ultimate future. We are a redeemed people, once scattered in every nation, now brought near through the Son. What an amazing and unique picture.

I was speaking with a community leader who had, from time to time, visited the church I pastor. He commented that Sunday service is like the United Nations. He was amazed at our diversity; we have at least sixty national groups represented. Of course, other churches have even more countries and people groups represented. But whatever our congregation's makeup, meeting together opens our eyes to that gathering to come of "a great multitude . . . crying out with a loud voice, 'Salvation belongs to our God . . . and to the Lamb!'" (Rev. 7:9–10).

Like leafing through the architectural plans of a grand building or walking through a model home, when we gather to worship, we witness a hope-filled vision of what is yet to come. What a feast for the eyes of faith.

Corporate worship opens our eyes to the truth of God's grand design of who we are and where we are going. Meeting regularly reinforces the truth that this world is not our true home, yet we are traveling companions together, headed for the same destination above.

Two, corporate worship allows us to hear God's Word proclaimed together. We can do so much remotely these days. We can take courses, do our work, attend seminars, and see friends and family online. But with all those capabilities, we know that being somewhere in person still matters. In certain experiences and relationships, we need to get ourselves there physically.

I remember the pressure in the corporate world during the global recession of 2009—at least in the United Kingdom, where we were at the time—upon people to reduce travel costs and attempt work remotely. Rather than fly overseas for a brief meeting and incur great cost, the push was to host virtual meetings instead.

But, of course, the trend did not seem to last too long. Professionals realized the value of personal encounters. Businesses realized the value of the handshake. *Presence was irreplaceably important.*

We can find great Bible teachings online and read the Scriptures for ourselves. But even so, meeting together as the people of God to hear the preaching of the Word is irreplaceably special.

Interestingly, when Paul sends instructions to his protégé Timothy in Ephesus regarding what he should prioritize in his ministry in that church, his chief instruction is to "preach the word" (2 Tim. 4:2). Above all else, preaching is Timothy's foremost and solemn responsibility.

Notice Paul's weighty charge to Timothy: "I charge you in the presence of God and of Christ Jesus, who is to judge the living and the dead, and by his appearing and his kingdom: preach the word; be ready in season and out of season; reprove, rebuke, and exhort, with complete patience and teaching" (vv. 1–2).

The verb *preach* in verse 2 is an important word: it means "to announce publicly as a herald, to declare." Paul underscores that Timothy can only do this kind of ministry when people gather to hear the spoken Word. Preaching only fits in that public context. Preaching is different from a Bible study or discussion of the Word. Preaching is a public proclamation, a declaration of truth. Notice how Paul outlines the task of preaching: "reprove, rebuke, and exhort with complete patience and teaching."

We all need to read the Word for ourselves; we need to talk about the Word with our families and other believers. All this is important. Nevertheless, we also need to hear the public declaration of the Word. We need those regular occasions when we listen together to what God says in the Scriptures and receive His challenge and exhortation.

When we hear the Word as a congregation week after week, it shapes us collectively. On Sunday morning, we hear together the same challenge and exhortation at the same time. Meeting face-to-face brings mutual accountability; we all know what we heard and what we need to do in response. This can only happen when we are gathered in one place, sharing the same experience, and hearing the same message. Listening to a podcast or video recording from elsewhere is not the same as gathering as the people of God to receive His Word and then going out with a shared sense of commitment to put that Word into practice.

When we think about meeting together in terms of ongoing transformation and accountability, we see the importance of not missing Sundays as a regular habit. But the reality is, of course, that many do not attend church weekly. While researching patterns of church attendance in North America, I read the comment that, whereas a couple of decades ago people would view themselves as regular church attendees if they attended three times a week, now people view themselves as regular attendees if they make it three times a month. And, of course, many people do not even manage that.

But friend, I want to encourage you to a higher standard. I am not invoking legalism but rather affirming that you and I need to hear the Word of God whether we are sitting in a pew or standing behind a pulpit. We need to be reminded of the truth; we need to be strengthened by the gospel of grace. We need to be challenged to respond.

Three, corporate worship is important because it allows us to speak and sing to one another. I commented earlier that we tend to assume the main purpose of gathering is to worship God. And of course, we do come together to worship God and magnify His name with heart and voice for who He is and what He has done in Christ. The *vertical dimension* of praise and thanksgiving to God is essential to corporate worship. Even so, when the New Testament addresses the importance of gathering, it often focuses even more on *horizontal dynamics* such as encouraging and edifying one another.

Perhaps one of the most important passages that speaks into our corporate gatherings is Hebrews 10:24–25:

> And let us consider how to stir up one another to love and good works, not neglecting to meet together, as is the habit of some, but encouraging one another, and all the more as you see the Day drawing near.

What does one of the key New Testament passages that speaks explicitly about the church's gathering say? *Do not neglect to meet together.* That is, do not let busyness or tiredness or work or sports keep you away from gathering with one another. Do not neglect meeting together, as is the habit of some. Moreover, consider how you can stir one another up to love and good works. Encourage one another.

If you ask the writer of Hebrews why it is important to be in church on Sunday morning, here is his Spirit-inspired answer, plain and simple: you need to be there to encourage your brothers and sisters in Christ.

Now, that is insightful. Because, if we think about a life of worship, we might envision many ways we can worship God on our own. We can worship Him in our prayers and in our times of Bible study. We can worship Him and honor Him in the way we speak to our family, treat our spouse, drive our car, and do our work.

But one aspect of worship that will only happen effectively and consistently when we gather face-to-face is encouragement. It is difficult to encourage our brothers and sisters in Christ if we do not see them consistently. Again, *being present with others is irreplaceably important.*

So, how do we do this work of encouragement? We might consider our conversations before and after the formal part of the service. Those can be key times of ministry.

But what about the service itself? How can we encourage one another in our Sunday services? To begin, let us recognize that when we recite a responsive reading, creed, or summary of our faith, we are speaking truth to one another. We encourage one another when we speak the truth aloud.

Moreover, we encourage one another through our singing. Paul exhorts his church family in Colossae: "Let the word of Christ dwell in you richly, teaching and admonishing one another in all wisdom, singing psalms and hymns and spiritual songs, with thankfulness in your hearts to God" (Col. 3:16). In other words, as a people filled with the Word of God, let us also minister God's Word to one another by singing with gratitude in our hearts to God.

Now, the implications of this verse are significant. Paul is indicating that our singing psalms, hymns, and spiritual songs is part of our ministry of the Word to one another. As we sing these rich truths—which must be truths from God's own Word, or we should not sing them—we not only express our gratitude to God on the vertical plane but also minister the Word to one another on the horizontal plane.

Paul makes the same point in Ephesians 5:15–21:

> Look carefully then how you walk, not as unwise but as wise, making the best use of the time, because the days are evil. Therefore do not be foolish, but understand what the will of the Lord is. And do not get drunk with wine, for that is debauchery, but be filled with the Spirit, addressing one another in psalms and hymns and spiritual songs, singing and making melody to the Lord with your heart, giving thanks always and for everything to God the Father in the name of our Lord Jesus Christ, submitting to one another out of reverence for Christ.

Paul observes that "the days are evil" (v. 16). The days were hard then, and they still are today. He says we need to use our time well, be wise, and understand the will of the Lord. We agree. He tells us to avoid debauchery and be filled with the Spirit. Then he adds what we are to do as wise, Spirit-filled people who maximize the time in these evil days: *we are to address one another in psalms and hymns and spiritual songs with thanksgiving in our hearts to God.*

Notice this horizontal element again. Paul emphasizes that we are ministering to one another as we worship God. We can worship God in song and praise Him *alone.* But worshipping Him *together* in song has the added benefit of encouraging and edifying one another. Ministering to one another is a significant part of gathering together, declares the New Testament.

When I stand and sing with my congregation "King Forevermore" or "Great Is Thy Faithfulness," I am encouraged to keep believing that God's Word is all true. As Christians, we can feel so isolated sometimes and can even wonder if we have been mistaken to believe that God's promises are true. Then we declare them in song together. I do not know about you, but I am helped immensely.

Or perhaps I am feeling condemned by sin, discouraged by my own failure, or doubting my ability to be forgiven. Then I gather with others on Sunday to sing, "Amazing grace! How sweet the sound, that saved a wretch like me!" Or "Amazing love! How can it be that Thou, my God, shouldst die for me?" As we rejoice in these truths together, I am encouraged to keep believing that they are true.

When we recognize that our singing involves this horizontal dimension, I believe we will change our approach to music as well.

What do I mean? I mentioned that we could imagine on Sunday morning that we are taking our seat to enjoy a performance. However, that expectation can undermine our ministry in song. Namely, if we believe we are attending a performance, each of us will focus on whether the music emanating from the platform suits us or if we are enjoying it.

Conversely, when I recognize that I am not only singing praises to God but also words that can edify those around me, I will respond to the music differently. I begin thinking, *Am I singing biblical truths that are going to encourage others? Is God's Word dwelling richly in me as I sing this song? Is my brother or sister going to be edified by its message? Will it resonate with them?*

These are particularly challenging questions to consider. In our church, we have people from every age group and cultural background. That may be true in your church too. We have people who love classical music, people who love country music, guitars, piano, drums, Charles Wesley hymns, and the latest modern worship song—and people who strongly dislike at least some of these things! Therefore, we try to create opportunities with any given song for a range of people to be edified and for a range of people to serve their brothers and sisters by singing songs that might warm their hearts.

Moreover, Scripture offers us guidance as we consider such opportunities and challenges with music selection. Paul does so at the end of Ephesians 5. We are to address one another in song, giving thanks to God and "submitting to one another out of reverence for Christ" (v. 21).

How fascinating. What does submitting to one another out of reverence for Christ have to do with our singing in church and with praise and worship? *It has everything to do with it.* Submitting to one another in this area is immensely difficult. Let us be honest. If there is one element in church life that straightens our backs and ignites our emotions, it is the music.

Music stirs something in the human heart like almost nothing else. So we feel strongly about it. I do, and I imagine many of you do.

But in our discussions about song selection, instruments, and genres, we easily overlook the fact that we are singing to serve one another and to minister to one another. That is what Scripture calls us to do. Thus, we choose to lay down our preferences in submission to one another and consider: How can I edify my brother? How can I minister to my sister? How can I bless them today?

For the one who would rather sing the newest release to the loudest drums and electric guitar, may I ask you: "What will it look like to serve your brother or sister who has a migraine just thinking about that?"

And for the one who would never by choice sing a song written after the year 1750 and would prefer hymns to the piano or—even better—organ and nothing else: What does it look like to serve individuals of a new generation who do not resonate so easily with that music but whom you long to encourage in their walk with the Lord?

Corporate worship can be challenging in many respects, yet it is also special and unique. In corporate worship, we see God's grand design, we hear His Word proclaimed, and we speak and sing to encourage one another. So we carve out time to meet on Sunday and protect our time together. We gather with one another out of reverence for Christ—out of reverence for the One who laid down His life for us—and to give ourselves in a real way to encourage one another. We do not neglect to meet together because we love Christ and His people. Truly, God has called us collectively to something profoundly good.

3

· · · · · · ·

Gathered to Serve

SINCE THE BEGINNING OF CREATION, GOD HAS BEEN gathering people for His glory and their good. He gathers us to Himself as His people and then to one another as a family. Knowing that we need others, God calls us to commit ourselves to our local church and to meet corporately to worship and encourage one another.

God also gathers us to serve. We express our love for Jesus and others when we serve Him with the gifts that He has given us. To explore this theme of service, we will look at a vitally important passage in Romans 12:1–8.

You may recall that Paul spends the first eleven chapters of Romans outlining the gospel. He speaks of the mercy and grace of God in Christ and shows us that we are made right with God through faith. That is, we are justified before God not because of anything we have done, but because Jesus died for us.

The start of Romans 12 is then a critical pivot point. Here, Paul tells us what living as gospel people looks like. He writes: "I appeal to you therefore, brothers, by the mercies of God, to present your bodies as a living sacrifice, holy and acceptable to God, which is your spiritual worship" (v. 1).

Serving God and His people in the work of the gospel is at the heart of the life of the local church. If you are actively engaged in serving, I hope this chapter will encourage you. If you have been on the sidelines, I hope you will discover that your service and gifts are meaningful and valuable. Your church family needs you and you need them. If you are considering becoming a Christian, I hope what follows will give you a realistic picture of true Christian community and devotion to Christ. Giving our lives in service to Christ and others is costly but beautiful.

So let us examine four principles of Christian service from the apostle Paul.

One, service flows from the mercies of God. Again, Paul says in Romans 12:1, "I appeal to you therefore, brothers, by the mercies of God."

Paul opens this pivotal section of Romans with these words. All he will write about practical Christian living here will flow from this appeal. He has much to say about the Christian life, but he begins with the theme of service. He clearly wants us to see that our service—the use of our gifts—flows directly from this understanding of the mercies of God.

So often in life, *we do things* in order to *get things*. Most people go to work (at least, in part) to get a paycheck. Students study hard for their exam to get a certain mark in order to get into a certain school or to get a certain job. We know about *doing stuff to get stuff.*

But in God's economy, when it comes to His saved people, the opposite is true. We do not serve in order to receive. We serve because we already have received: "I appeal to you therefore, brothers, by the mercies of God" (v. 1).

To be shown mercy is to be spared something unwelcome that we rightly deserve.

At the outset of Romans, Paul declares the unsettling news that God is angry with sinful humanity. In 1:18, he observes: "For the wrath of God is revealed from heaven against all ungodliness and unrighteousness of men, who by their unrighteousness suppress the truth." We should recognize, honor, and worship our Creator, but we have not naturally done that. Instead, we have turned to our own way and lived as we pleased. The Bible calls that attitude of heart and the behaviors that flow from it "sin." Paul goes on in Romans to tell us just how seriously God takes sin, writing in 6:23 that "the wages of sin is death."

God's punishment for sin is death. Rebellion against the Creator is always a capital offense. Death is what we all deserve. Moreover, Scripture says this is not just physical death but a spiritual death that endures beyond the grave: a lostness, an enduring punishment, and a separation from the blessings of God.

But, as Paul takes special care to show us in the book of Romans, God has made another way for all who will trust in Him. In sending His Son to live the perfect life and then die the death we deserve, God transfers our guilt to Him. At the same time, Christ transfers to us His perfect record and His righteous standing before God. It is a glorious exchange.

Through the life and death of Jesus, God shows us mercy if we trust in Him. He does not treat us as our sins deserve. Romans 6:23: "For the wages of sin is death, but the free gift of God is eternal life in Christ Jesus our Lord."

Perhaps serving Jesus feels burdensome to you. Perhaps carving out time and energy seems too much to ask. Understandably, we can all get weary. But may I ask you: Have you lost sight of the mercies of God in Christ? Have you forgotten what you deserve, what Jesus has paid, and what He has given you instead?

You may remember that wonderful moment in Victor Hugo's *Les Misérables* when Jean Valjean, the runaway thief, is caught by the police. He was a fugitive, yet an old bishop kindly sheltered him one night. Valjean returns the bishop's hospitality by stealing his fine household silver and running off into the shadows. The police catch him and drag him before the bishop for confirmation of the crime. But instead of condemning Valjean, the bishop chides him for forgetting to take his valuable candlesticks as well and tells the police that the silver is his gift to him.

Then the bishop whispers those memorable words to him, "Do not forget, never forget, that you have promised to use this money in becoming an honest man. . . . Jean Valjean, my brother, you no longer belong to evil, but to good. It is your soul that I buy from you."[1]

As the story progresses, we discover that an older Valjean has indeed been transformed by this act of kindness and leads a vastly different life because of it.

Victor Hugo's captivating story mirrors beautifully what Paul says here in Romans. The grace and mercy of God showcased in Romans 1–11 is meant to produce transformed people in chapter 12. The mercy of God is what motivates and moves us to serve. Paul appeals to us by the mercies of God.

If you are struggling to find any motivation to serve God and His people, may I ask you again: Have you lost sight of the

---

1. Victor Hugo, *Les Misérables*, translated by Isabel F. Hapgood (New York: Thomas Y. Crowell & Co., 1887), chapter 12, online from Project Gutenburg.

mercies of God? Have you forgotten what you and I rightly deserve, and have you forgotten what God has done for us in Christ? I believe that only when we take hold of this truth and its wonder fills our hearts will we be ready to serve God and His people joyfully and willingly.

Service flows from the mercies of God.

Two, service flows from personal sacrifice. Look at verse 1 again: "I appeal to you therefore, brothers, by the mercies of God, *to present your bodies as a living sacrifice*, holy and acceptable to God, which is your spiritual worship" (emphasis added).

We live in a time when we expect most things in life to be convenient and comfortable. In the age of drive-through Starbucks, we do not want to leave our car to get our coffee. In the age of Alexa and Siri, we do not want to have to flip a switch or push a button to get our music or our news. In the age of Amazon and Wayfair, we do not want to leave our house to do our shopping. In the age of Uber Eats, we resent having to drive all the way to the restaurant to have our food cooked for us. Inconvenience and discomfort are simply no longer acceptable or compatible with our lifestyle.

Now, many of these conveniences are blessings of the modern era, and I am certainly not complaining. However, the danger comes when we import that convenience-culture attitude to our service of the Lord Jesus in the work of the gospel. That is, when we are asked to serve or opportunities are presented to us to serve, often we ask the convenience question. I know I do all too readily, and I expect you do the same. *Will this be convenient for me? Will it be comfortable? Will it be costly? Will it get in the way of other things I would like to do?*

So, *I appeal to you therefore, brothers, by the mercies of God, to present your bodies as a living sacrifice, holy and acceptable to God.*

Jesus gave Himself as a sacrifice for us. In view of His mercies, we offer ourselves as living sacrifices and give up our rights, our preferences, and our conveniences. We make ourselves wholly available for His service with no claim on our own time, energy, plans, or ambitions. We give everything over to Jesus Christ.

Yes, giving our lives to Christ and to others is costly. But it is also beautiful.

I understand that we instinctively ask such questions when we are called upon to serve. We wonder: *Will I enjoy it? Will it be rewarding and convenient?* Well, it may be some of those things some of the time. But sometimes service will be costly, painful, draining, and difficult.

I was in our church building on a Thursday night and bumped into a few volunteers who are here each week to help with our children's Bible club. I am certain that some of those individuals left home for work before seven a.m., and now at eight p.m., they are at church. I know they could have enjoyed an evening at home and an early night.

I think of a missionary family we communicate with regularly. Knowing their situation, I cannot begin to calculate the cost for them in bringing the gospel to the needy country where they serve. Besides the financial cost, they endure the cost to their wider family in being at a distance, the cost of being cultural outsiders, the cost of a lower quality education for their children, the cost of loneliness. The cost for them in serving Jesus is *immense*.

We could think of countless stories throughout church history of those who have given their lives serving in difficult places and in situations of real persecution. Over and again, history reminds us that the gospel goes out and the church is built on the back of personal sacrifice.

Whether you are called to full-time, vocational ministry or you are called to serve within the local church alongside life in the community and the secular workplace, your calling is going to come with a cost. Serving will be difficult sometimes; it is, by its nature, a sacrifice.

So let me ask you as I ask myself: "Are you serving the Lord Jesus and His people as a living sacrifice today? Are you serving simply as it fits your lifestyle and suits your preferences? Are you serving at all?"

Service flows from personal sacrifice.

Three, service flows from sober self-assessment. When we first come to Christ, we must learn a whole new way of thinking and an entirely new value system and outlook on the world and on ourselves.

In fact, immediately after Paul calls us to give our lives as a living sacrifice to Jesus, he urges us: "Do not be conformed to this world [a world that deplores the idea of sacrifice, discomfort, inconvenience—a world that is fixated on self—do not be conformed to this world], but be transformed by the renewal of your mind, that by testing you may discern what is the will of God, what is good and acceptable and perfect" (Rom. 12:2).

We need a transformation in our thinking. Our mind needs to break free of the world's mold and be made new as God's Spirit works through His Word. And in no area do we need a greater transformation in our thinking than in our own self-assessment and view of ourselves. In fact, Paul says in verse 3: "For by the grace given to me I say to everyone among you not to think of himself more highly than he ought to think, but to think with sober judgment, each according to the measure of faith that God has assigned."

Now, there is no question that many people struggle with low self-esteem and their own worth as people made in God's image and precious in His sight. This is a real struggle for many and may even be your struggle. To these thoughts and feelings Scripture offers answers that increase our dignity and remind us of our worth before God. The Bible tells us we are made in His image, redeemed by the blood of His Son, and precious in His sight. These are important truths to guide and encourage us.

But at the same time, we must recognize that the nature of sin is characteristically to drive us to pride and to arrogance. Something about the essence of sin leans in that direction. Think back to the garden of Eden. Adam and Eve were tempted to believe they knew better than God, as if God were holding back from them things they would enjoy. They were tempted with the thought that they could become like God, knowing good from evil, and it was arrogance and pride. We are the same today. Whenever we reject *God's* way and go *our* way, we make a declaration of willful independence, a declaration that we know best.

And so, all of us face a constant temptation and inclination in our fallen nature to think too highly of ourselves. We are prone to overestimate our own wisdom and even our own importance.

After about fifteen years off the slopes, I recently had my first fresh experience of downhill skiing. I enjoyed getting back on skis and was relieved to find that I still had some memory of how to do it and was able to progress beyond the bunny hill.

As I have been thinking of getting back into skiing, I have been mindful of the need for equipment. My parents still had my old skis in their basement that I got when I was about fifteen years old. I was thinking I could dust them off and load into them again just fine. They were a fluorescent green with pink accenting—vintage 1990s style—and straight and pointy, not like those curvy new ones. I thought they would be fine. I remember how they were pretty nice skis back in 1997.

But I realized I was probably in dangerous territory when I talked about getting them back from my parents and my mother basically told me that, yes, I could have them, but I probably should not be seen dead using those skis (or something to that effect). When your mother tells you that you are about to commit a dangerous fashion faux pas, you know you are probably heading for some significant embarrassment.

So I took the hint and decided to start shopping online for used skis. I combed through scores of ads that looked appealing. However, one problem in buying used is that not everyone tells you the size very clearly, and you cannot just tell the size of a ski from the pictures.

But one person did a sensible thing in his online post. He not only specified the length of the ski but also included a picture of the ski lined up next to a measuring tape so you could see the size for yourself. How practical and helpful.

At the end of verse 3, Paul tells us we should think of ourselves "with sober judgment, each according to the measure of faith that God has assigned." Now, we could conclude that Paul means God has given some people more faith than others, and he is talking here about a *quantity* of faith. That is, if you have more if it, your self-assessment will be more accurate.

More likely, though, Paul is saying that faith—gospel faith in Christ crucified and risen again, or *the faith*—is the measuring stick by which we measure ourselves and view ourselves. Like the skis in the photo with the measuring tape, or like a child standing next to a growth chart in a doctor's office, we picture ourselves standing next to the measure of the gospel.

What does it look like to measure ourselves by the measure of faith? To begin, the gospel tells us that we were ruined sinners destined for destruction yet redeemed by the blood of Christ. The gospel tells us that, at great cost, and for no merit of our own, Jesus has made us part of His family and part of His body.

And so, measuring ourselves by the measure of the gospel, here is how we see ourselves now according to Romans 12:4–5: "For as in one body we have many members, and the members do not all have the same function, so we, though many, are one body in Christ, and individually members one of another."

As a Canadian, I inhabit a society of rugged individualists. We prize our freedom and autonomy. Our outlook throughout the Western world over the last couple of hundred years has been shaped by the dream of self-determination, liberty, and the pursuit of our own ends and our own happiness. As has been said, ours is the age of the iPhone, the iWatch, the iPad, and the "I" everything.

That is the culture we inhabit. But when we are redeemed by Christ and then put ourselves on the altar as living sacrifices available entirely to Him, our identity and outlook change.

When I was a kid, my dad took me for a tour of the General Motors car plant in Oshawa, Ontario. The Oshawa plant is Ontario's historic piece of a great modern phenomenon: mass production of the automobile. Of course, much changed over the course of that factory's life as car manufacturing has been revolutionized, and much has changed since our visit thirty years ago. The product produced at Oshawa is now the result of a global collaboration between workers in countless places preparing components for this one single product made up of so many disparate parts. The average modern car is made up of thirty thousand different parts that come together to make that unified, gleaming car that rolls off the line.

When we come to Christ from many different backgrounds, nationalities, and places, He brings us together as part of one body. And, within that body, each one of us has our own special and vital function.

In coming to Christ, we become part of something greater, beautiful, and purposeful. Our identity is no longer all about us, our dreams, or our plans. According to the measure of the gospel, our identity is now bound up with being part of the body of Christ.

Christian service flows from this vital self-understanding. We are not all about the "I" anymore. We are all about Christ and His people; we are all about being the body together.

Now when we look in the mirror, we may not be seeing the measuring stick of the gospel as clearly as we should. You and I may still be viewing ourselves through that worldly framework where the "I" is king, where my rights and my preferences and my plans and my reputation and my goals are all-important. If that is the case, we need to be transformed by the renewing of our minds through the Word of God as His Spirit works within.

You see, if we approach Christian service within the church or ministry with the world's outlook—with an outlook focused on ourselves—we will be a terrible liability. We will look on ministry opportunities, and we will ask, "How does this fit in with *my plans* and *my agenda*? How will this showcase *my gifts* and *my abilities*? How will this fit in with *my calendar*?"

How refreshing when, from time to time, individuals here in the church family approach me or other pastors and say, "I want to serve. How can I be of use? I am available. Please let me know if there are ways I can get involved."

That should be the attitude of all our hearts: I am a servant of Jesus Christ, redeemed by the blood of the Lamb. I am nothing on my own but have been made new in Christ. How can I serve my Savior and His people?

Serving flows from sober judgment.

Four, serving flows from gifts of grace. Verses 6–8 of Romans 12 says: "Having gifts that differ according to the grace given to us, let us use them: if prophecy, in proportion to our faith; if service, in our serving; the one who teaches, in his teaching; the one who exhorts, in his exhortation; the one who contributes, in generosity; the one who leads, with zeal; the one who does acts of mercy, with cheerfulness."

When you begin a new job, you may be given certain tools needed for the role. Maybe it is a uniform, a company vehicle, a computer, or a phone.

The Bible teaches that when we come to Christ and receive new life in Him and join His family, He gives us gifts that we are to use in His service. Out of His grace and undeserved kindness, He gives each of us gifts, though not all the same gifts. Remember the image of a body; each part of the body does not function the same way. Paul speaks elsewhere of different functions (see 1 Cor. 12), but the simple point is that we have been given gifts to serve.

Hence, having been given certain gifts, he states clearly in verse 6, "let us use them."

God is never deficient in giving His gifts to His church. He gives them freely of His grace. All believers have them. If you are a follower of Jesus, born again of His Spirit, He has given you gifts to use in His service; you can be sure of that. So, if as a church we are struggling to find people to serve or we have gaps in our ministry, here must be the problem: God's people are just not using the gifts He has given. God has distributed the needed gifts, but we are not using them.

Scripture identifies a variety of gifts including speaking, proclaiming, and applying the Word of God, serving in practical ways, exhorting and encouraging the saints, giving generously, leading, and performing acts of mercy.

Do you know what gifts God has given you? Ultimately, understanding your gifts will likely involve other believers helping you discern them and affirming you in them. Or maybe you do not have a gift you think you have, and brothers and sisters need to gently inform you that you are not the operatic singer you might think you are. Maybe you are not the teacher you hoped you would be. Maybe you have a gift you have never recognized, but others around you see it clearly, waiting to be used for God's glory.

As you recognize your gifts, here are the next questions: Are you using the gifts God has given you? Are you making yourself available to serve? Are you placing yourself on the altar as a living sacrifice and playing your part in the body of Christ?

We live in challenging times, even dark times. There is no shortage of gospel work to do. God is opening all kinds of doors of opportunity before us. As Jesus says, "the harvest is plentiful" (Matt. 9:37). But the limiting factor is always the same: *workers*. Challenging times require workers who will sacrificially serve in the work of the gospel, who will sacrificially make space in their lives. Gospel work may involve limiting career ambitions, choosing not to pursue some hobbies or sports, or making other difficult adjustments to be available to serve in the body of Christ.

Imagine what would happen if each of us in our local church would say, "Lord Jesus, I am available. How would You use me?" And then if we would say to one another: "How can I serve?" Imagine what could be done; imagine what the Lord might do.

But if we are to do that, ultimately, we will need to have our values calibrated by the gospel. We will need to have such a sense of wonder at the mercies of God that we gladly lay down all we are to serve Him in whatever way He calls us with whatever gifts He gives.

In coming to Christ, we become part of something greater, beautiful, and purposeful. Giving our lives in service to Him and others is costly but beautiful.

4

· · · · · · ·

Gathered to Give

A PASTOR IN THE CITY WHERE I GREW UP WAS WELL-KNOWN for his exhortations to his congregation to contribute financially. I do not suggest he was being manipulative; he just had a particular gift for this, and the church was able to be generous in wider kingdom work as a result.

One day a child we knew managed to swallow a coin. Her father quipped as he recounted the incident, "Instead of waiting at the emergency room, we wondered if we should just take her up to see pastor so-and-so. We hear that he can get money out of anybody."

Of course, no one wants to be pressured into giving money to the church. However, when you look at the New Testament, you observe that Jesus and the apostles spoke often about money. You see readily that our use of money is a central part of our Christian discipleship.

Paul addresses the subject of giving in 2 Corinthians chapters 8 and 9. Some Christians in the church in Jerusalem are facing real financial needs, and Paul mentions in several of his letters that he is collecting funds from other churches to help. He has mentioned it already in 1 Corinthians, and evidently the Christians at Corinth have committed to help. Now Paul is urging them to follow up and prepare their gift.

Paul is addressing a concrete situation; he has a practical purpose in mind. Nevertheless, as he teaches and prepares these Christians to meet a particular need, he offers them and us the theological foundation of giving.

So let us consider three key principles for Christian giving from this key passage of Scripture.

One, Christian giving is shaped by grace. In 2 Corinthians 8:9, Paul grounds our theology of giving in the grace of God: "For you know the grace of our Lord Jesus Christ, that though he was rich, yet for your sake he became poor, so that you by his poverty might become rich."

The astounding grace of God in Christ shapes our giving in every way.

Stories of wealthy people committing themselves to philanthropy are inspirational. Each of us can probably think readily of some notable philanthropists who have become famous for their generosity and who have made real contributions to their communities and to important causes around the world. Rarely, though, do any of these wealthy philanthropists make themselves *poor* through their giving.

Knowing this, I was fascinated to learn of the story of Chuck Feeney, the late multibillionaire *who did make himself poor*. He decided to give away his entire fortune to charity. In his latter years, he lived in a modest rental apartment in San Francisco, owning no car or luxuries of any kind, having quietly given away his $8 billion-dollar fortune because "it was the right thing to do."[2]

To me, that is impressive, but going from billionaire to modest retiree has *nothing* on the journey Jesus took for us.

Just consider Jesus's wealth: the eternal Son of God in splendor with His Father—with hosts of angels at His beck and call, with power supreme over all creation—existing in glory, bliss, and blessedness on high. And how poor did He become? He became man, born as a baby, born in a stable, living in humility, facing rejection and scorn, dying on a cross for my sin and yours.

---

2. Robert D. McFadden, "Charles Feeney, Who Made a Fortune and Then Gave It Away, Dies at 92," *The New York Times*, October 13, 2023, https://www.nytimes.com/2023/10/09/business/charles-f-feeney-dead.html.

Moreover, as Jesus poured Himself out for us by taking on our sin and guilt and dying for sinners like us, *He made us rich.* He gave us His perfect record before the Father. He offered us forgiveness and life. He gave us a fresh start, a new family, and an eternal home in heaven.

For you know the grace of our Lord Jesus Christ, that though he was rich, yet for your sake he became poor, so that you by his poverty might become rich.

Paul has much to say in these two chapters about the practicalities of giving. But what is the foundation of his appeal? He highlights the generosity and grace of Jesus Christ. You see, we will only be interested in giving and moved to true generosity when we understand that the Lord of glory became poor for us. The Son of God poured Himself out in order that we who had nothing might receive everything and we who deserve nothing might inherit spiritual riches beyond measure.

A couple of the educational institutions I have been through write to me from time to time in their efforts to fundraise. I am sympathetic to their needs and do not mind receiving the invitations to give. Even so, I notice something consistent in the fundraising of non-Christian charities: they often offer incentives to give by way of name recognition. If you give so much, you join the bronze club; a bit more, the silver club; or even more, the gold—and your name will be published in their magazine or engraved on a wall. Clearly, that recognition motivates some people.

But within the church of Jesus Christ, within the family of God, we would be rightly embarrassed to receive recognition of that kind. Indeed, we know we give only as a small response to what we have received. We were poor, and in Christ, we have been made spiritually rich beyond our wildest dreams. God has gathered and nourished us by His grace and gives us the privilege to extend His grace to a needy world.

We give in response to grace. Indeed, it would be fair to suggest that our giving will reflect our grasp of grace. Paul is being intentional in verse 9 in linking the gospel and the gift of the Son of God to the practicalities of giving. The two are related, he underscores. The Son of God has poured Himself out for us in painful, costly, and sacrificial ways. When we understand His profound grace, we will instinctively respond by pouring ourselves out in costly, sacrificial ways that include our finances.

That connection may not be comfortable, but it is obvious. So let me ask you: "What is your grasp of grace?" And, once you answer that question, let me then ask you this: "Will your answer be corroborated by your bank statement?"

We can sing "O How I Love Jesus" or "Jesus, Thank You." We can sing of God's grace with gusto and hands lifted high, but would our bank statement confirm the expression of our lips?

We give to the Lord's work because of grace. But I want us to see that this dynamic is not simply responsive; that is, Jesus has done something for us, we are grateful, and so we give. Rather, grace drives our giving in a deeper way. Our giving is not only a response to the grace of God but also an *expression* of the grace of God at work in our lives.

Notice Paul's report of the Macedonian churches in 2 Corinthians 8:1–2: "We want you to know, brothers, about *the grace of God* that has been given among the churches of Macedonia, for in a severe test of affliction, their abundance of joy and their extreme poverty have overflowed in a wealth of generosity on their part" (emphasis added).

God's grace has moved a people who are not rich to be generous. Thus, Paul is expectant that God's grace will be at work similarly in the Corinthians. He continues: "Accordingly, we urged Titus that as he had started, so he should complete among you *this act of grace.* But as you excel in everything—in faith, in speech, in knowledge, in all earnestness, and in our love for you—see that you excel in this *act of grace* also" (vv. 6–7, emphasis added).

Giving is an act of grace. But what is "grace" in Paul's language and in Scripture? Grace is what God freely gives *to His people* and achieves *through His people.* Grace is what God does in His kindness. Grace comes from God, not from us. Grace is achieved by Him and not by us.

Paul says that the financial giving of the Corinthian Christians will be the work of God in and through them. As they give, they will be instruments of God Himself to extend His grace to others. God is the source, the motivator, the enabler.

This truth runs through Paul's entire discussion in this section of 2 Corinthians. He encourages generosity again in chapter 9:

> Each one must give as he has decided in his heart, not reluctantly or under compulsion, for God loves a cheerful giver. And God is able to make all grace abound to you, so that having all sufficiency in all things at all times, you may abound in every good work. As it is written, "He has distributed freely, he has given to the poor; his righteousness endures forever." He who supplies seed to the sower and bread for food will supply and multiply your seed for sowing and increase the harvest of your righteousness. (vv. 7–10)

As you seek to be generous, God will make His grace abound to you. He will supply all that is needed for you to be generous. In His grace, he will enable your acts of grace.

One of the leading Christian philanthropists in Canada in the mid-twentieth century was a home builder in Toronto named Robert McClintock. McClintock quietly supported gospel work in Canada and around the world. He was from a humble background, having immigrated from Ireland as a child, but his business became successful. He built large swathes of the growing suburbs of eastern Toronto in the 1950s through the 1970s. He once commented in his down-to-earth way that, as the Lord provided wealth for him, he tried to shovel it out again to give it to gospel work. He said he soon discovered that the Lord had the bigger shovel! His point was that, as he gave, the Lord continued to provide for him so that he could continue to give.

The farming imagery Paul uses here in these verses is significant. Think about the work of a farmer. Now, who grows crops; that is, *who actually causes them to grow?* If we believe in a Creator, we believe He is the one who makes it happen. But what about the farmer? The farmer has the privilege of participating in a real way in the Creator's own work. He sows seed, but the seed comes from God, and God is the one who makes it grow.

You and I write a check, put money in the offering plate, or make an online transfer. Even so, where does the money come from? We might say we earned it through our job. Yes, but where do we receive the strength and gifts to work? Additionally, when the money is given to supply the needs of the saints and to promote the work of the gospel, who brings forth the spiritual fruit?

I think we can see the argument Paul is making. This is all God's work. It is all His grace. Paul wants us to understand that we are given the privilege of being participants in His grace.

Christian giving is shaped by grace from beginning to end in every way.

Two, Christian giving is marked by generosity. Notice with me how Paul introduces his argument here in 2 Corinthians 9:7–10. He writes in verse 6, "The point is this: whoever sows sparingly will also reap sparingly, and whoever sows bountifully will also reap bountifully. Each one must give as he has decided in his heart, not reluctantly or under compulsion, for God loves a cheerful giver."

I guess it would be possible for a farmer at the start of the season to decide that he would only sow seed on a portion of his land or that he would sow less seed to make it stretch a little further. He might do that out of laziness; he might do it in an effort to save money. But we all know what will happen in the end: the harvest will be smaller. The crop will be reduced according to what the farmer has sown.

We receive a spiritual harvest from giving to the Lord's work and sharing what we have with the wider family of God. Nevertheless, the scale of the harvest to come depends on how we sow at the front end.

Paul knows human nature well enough to know that some people will be inclined to act like that farmer: they will be inclined to sow sparingly when it comes to their money. He wants to urge us to sow bountifully, to put down lots of seed and expect a great harvest at the end.

Now, at this point, you may be wanting Paul to lay it out for us. "Give us a number, Paul. What do you mean by bountiful sowing? Give me a dollar amount or at least a percentage to work with here."

And to our disappointment or perhaps relief, Paul does not do that. Rather, he offers us freedom: "Each one must give as he has decided in his heart, not reluctantly or under compulsion, for God loves a cheerful giver" (v. 7).

Paul commends to us generosity throughout these two chapters in 2 Corinthians. The Macedonians gave with a "wealth of generosity," he tells us in 2 Corinthians 8:2. Likewise, God can enable the Corinthians to be generous (see 9:11). He expects their contribution will indeed be generous (9:13). Christian giving is to be marked by generosity.

Even so, Paul knows that generous giving requires thought and planning instead of merely digging in our pocket or purse when the plate comes around to find what is there between the Tic Tacs and the car keys. No, that will never make for a generous gift. To be generous, we must prayerfully decide in our heart what will be done and then carry it out faithfully.

In the Old Testament, the people of God were called to give a tithe, a tenth of their income as a foundation for their giving. In the New Testament, that is not set down as a rule, but many Christians over time have taken that to be a good pattern to follow—or, at least, a good starting point.

In 1 Corinthians 16:2, when Paul first instructs the church to prepare for this gift, he writes: "On the first day of every week, each of you is to put something aside and store it up, as he may prosper."

Each week, put something aside according to your prosperity—that is, in keeping with your wealth and your income. Our giving should reflect what the Lord has entrusted to us. Some will find it difficult to give 10 percent of income in times of financial strain. It is wise to note that there is no law or rule requiring it. We have freedom; we do not live under law. With that freedom, we know that others could give 20 percent or more without much strain, as we ourselves might do similarly in another season.

Whatever the number, the idea of a proportionate gift implies that this should reflect our wealth and income in some tangible way.

Ottawa, where I live, is at the top of the income bracket within Canada, and Canada is, in turn, one of the most prosperous countries on earth. By and large, when we stand next to brothers and sisters in Christ around the globe, Christians in our community are some of the wealthiest Christians in the world. That is the demographic reality; the numbers do not lie. By any objective measure, our community is highly privileged. And for many readers, the truth is that you likely are too. Now, your personal financial situation may be difficult at the moment, and I do not intend to minimize any challenges you may be facing. But, overall, we generally are a people in a strong position to give.

Given the wealth of our societies, perhaps not surprisingly, countries like Canada, the United States, and Great Britain have something of a culture of giving. Non-Christians give to charity sometimes generously. A culture of charity in wealthy nations is commendable and right. But, as Christians, we do not view *charity* in the typical sense because we are a people, first and foremost, transformed by grace. God has gathered us as His people by His grace. Our lives are now shaped by His grace as He works in us by His spirit. So our giving will be of a different order entirely from those around us.

What will it look like for you and for me, as materially privileged people, to sow bountifully and give willingly and cheerfully?

It should look like a kind of generosity the world around us does not see. It should look like we are making some distinctive life choices—saying no to some things we could have, foregoing some experiences we could enjoy, and doing so to sow for a harvest to come.

We do not bankrupt ourselves to give. We are not called to go into debt to give. We do not go without home or food.

In fact, Paul speaks of fairness in 2 Corinthians 8:12–14:

> For if the readiness is there, it is acceptable according to what a person has, not according to what he does not have. For I do not mean that others should be eased and you burdened, but that as a matter of fairness your abundance at the present time should supply their need, so that their abundance may supply your need, that there may be fairness.

We give as the Lord enables us to give. Our giving will look different for each of us. Again, we have no rule or law set down for us. But if we are honest, in a wealthy society like ours, God has put us in a privileged position where we can give in significant ways.

Changing our way of life to do this can be fearsome. Planning to give will mean that we need to set out our giving priorities before we set out our other priorities. As the foundation of our budgeting and our financial planning, we need first and foremost to determine before the Lord what we will give. Then, we figure out the other pieces of our finances around our giving. If we do everything else first and give what is left over, we will likely not give much at all. That is the reality. Nonetheless, giving first and planning everything else second can be fearful because we can worry that our giving and generosity will drive us into financial trouble or impoverish us.

However, the flow of Paul's argument tells us that God provides for us and sustains us as we give. He is able to give grace to us in such a way that we will have sufficiency (v. 8). We will not become dependent on others and destitute through prayerful, generous giving. No, God will provide for us so that we can abound in giving. He is the God who supplies seed to the sower and bread to the eater. As we seek to sow, He will multiply that seed for sowing so that there will be a harvest of deeds of generosity done in righteousness (v. 10)—a harvest of the deeds God has enabled by grace.

Indeed, take to heart this promise: "You will be enriched in every way to be generous in every way" (v. 11).

This is not a promise that if we give away money, we are going to become rich. That idea has been preached to manipulate people into giving out of a desire for riches: if you write a big check, you will enjoy wealth and health as an added bonus. That is not what Paul is saying here. Paul is saying that as we give, God provides for our needs so that we can keep on giving. I think that is what Robert McClintock was expressing when he said that God had the bigger shovel. He found that as he gave money away, the Lord continued to provide for him so that he could keep on giving.

Moreover, the Lord not only provides for our material needs as we give but also enriches us in every way (v. 11), which means *spiritually as well*. Our own practical righteousness and our godliness grow as we give. It does us good to give. As we participate in giving, the Lord grows within us the practical godliness to move and motivate us to give—and to give with the generosity that marks true Christian giving.

And so, I wonder: Is giving a practical reality in your life? Are you sowing bountifully? Are you giving willingly, generously, and cheerfully?

We read in 2 Corinthians 9:7 that "God loves a cheerful giver." Cheerful, generous giving reflects the heart of God. He loves to see that spirit of generosity within us.

One of our children earned his first income recently when a neighbor paid him five dollars to shovel snow outside his house. He had recently heard of a gospel opportunity in another country. When he came home from shoveling with five dollars in hand, he told us he was giving his earnings to this missions project so that people could hear about Jesus.

Now, our young son does not have a mortgage or car payments to worry about. But that five dollars still meant a lot to him. I was challenged and encouraged by his generosity, spontaneity, and the cheerfulness with which he gave.

We adults have perhaps a more complicated relationship with money with a mortgage, taxes, car payments, and the rest. I wonder if you and I have lost the simplicity of a child's gift—that spontaneous, cheerful, generous instinct that reflects well what Paul is talking about here. Scripture teaches us that Christian giving is shaped by grace, and Christian giving is marked by generosity.

Three, Christian giving is for God's glory. One of the biggest trends in fundraising in recent years has been the opportunity for donors to have buildings named after them in exchange for massive gifts. Hedge fund manager Stephen Schwarzman got his name on the main building of the New York Public Library for giving 100 million U.S. dollars. John Harvard had a school named after him in 1639 for leaving the college four hundred books and about eight hundred British pounds. That sounds like a good deal in today's economy.

Without attributing selfish motives to these or other donors, we must recognize that we all are tempted to care about our own reputation more than we should. The offer of a bit of fame and glory would appeal to anyone. But giving to the Lord and His work is about something entirely different; it is about *God's glory*—His reputation, His praise, and His honor.

The particular giving project that Paul is speaking of in chapter 9 is contributing to the practical needs of the Christians in Jerusalem. As Paul considers delivering gifts from other Christians in Corinth to these Christians in Jerusalem, he wants these donors to imagine the results: "For the ministry of this service is not only supplying the needs of the saints but is also overflowing in many thanksgivings to God" (v. 12). That is, the practical needs are met. But beyond that, there is an overflow in thanksgiving to God Himself, says Paul in verse 13: "By their approval of this service, they will glorify God because of your submission that comes from your confession of the gospel of Christ, and the generosity of your contribution for them and for all others."

Now, why does the glory go to God? Why does the gift of the Corinthian Christians cause the Jerusalem Christians to praise and thank God? They see that this generosity flows from a submission to God that comes from a "confession of the gospel of Christ" (v. 12). They recognize that the generosity flows from the "grace of God" that is upon the giver (v. 14).

This brings us full circle; it takes us back to the beginning. The believer's generosity brings glory to God because it comes through the grace of God. And for that reason, Paul ends his discussion of giving as he does in verse 15: "Thanks be to God for his inexpressible gift!"

The glory goes to God because all giving flows from His gift. He has given a gift the likes of which the world has never seen, a gift that can never be repaid or outgiven: the inexpressible gift of the Son of God for ruined sinners, helpless and hopeless people, even people like us.

I wonder where you are in this whole matter of giving. Are you giving to the Lord's work and making money available to meet the needs of other believers and gospel workers around the world? Are you making money available for the ministry that goes on within your local church walls and beyond, that Jesus might be proclaimed, that His gospel might go to a needy world, and that praise and thanksgiving and honor might be returned to God?

Maybe you are a committed giver. You have that grace and are living it out. Be encouraged in what you are doing and keep going.

Maybe you give, but it is not something you have carefully considered for some time. Maybe it is time to pray through your giving again and to make sure real generosity and true sacrifice are involved.

Maybe you give something, but, if you are being honest, you know it is token, haphazard, not proportionate to your income. The Word of God prompts you to look at that again and to grow in this grace.

Maybe you have never made a start in giving. Maybe you are a fairly new Christian or a Christian that has never really heard teaching on this, or you have been avoiding the subject just a little. Perhaps today will be the start of that *grace* in your life and the start of that discipline.

Giving is part of experiencing the grace of God in Christ. Giving is central to the way we extend that grace to others, to brothers and sisters in need, to those who have never heard. Giving is at the heart of God's plan to use our lives for His glory.

5

· · · · · · ·

Gathered to the Table

I ONCE HEARD A STORY ABOUT A CHURCH IN THE CANADIAN prairies that may or may not be based entirely on myth. If you visited this church in winter, you would observe something strange. At the start of the service, everyone would sit on one side of the church, but midway through, everyone would spontaneously stand up in unison and move to the other side.

Now, if you asked many of their church members why they did this, they might not be able to tell you. But a few older ones would tell you exactly why: when this little frame church was first built, it was heated by a wood stove on one side of the room. At the start of the service, everyone would huddle near the wood stove until it warmed up. Then, when it got too hot, they would move over to the other side of the room. The wood stove was long gone, but the tradition remained because people just got into the habit.

I imagine we might also do things in our own local church out of tradition or habit without fully understanding why we do them. We might easily do several things out of subconscious reflex and without much consideration.

One custom celebrated by the church worldwide is the Lord's Supper or Communion. Of course, like all traditions, Communion can become something we do by reflex or habit, without careful consideration. Indeed, the danger for us is that participating in this regular observance becomes empty of significance because of its sheer familiarity.

Why do we to take part in Communion and make a regular priority of it in our gatherings? In this chapter, we will look to the Word of God to deepen our understanding of Communion and consider two prerequisites as we gather at the Table.

We begin first with a crisis in the early church. Often within the letters of the New Testament, you will notice a writer comments on particular concerns because he knows problems need to be addressed. That is certainly the case in 1 Corinthians 11. Paul has heard of troubles in Corinth on various fronts, and he has spoken to some of them earlier in his letter. Even so, a particular problem impacts the Lord's Supper; thus, before teaching on the Supper, Paul communicates that he is aware of a crisis at Corinth.

> But in the following instructions I do not commend you, because when you come together it is not for the better but for the worse. For, in the first place, when you come together as a church, I hear that there are divisions among you. And I believe it in part, for there must be factions among you in order that those who are genuine among you may be recognized. When you come together, it is not the Lord's supper that you eat. For in eating, each one goes ahead with his own meal. One goes hungry, another gets drunk. What! Do you not have houses to eat and drink in? Or do you despise the church of God and humiliate those who have nothing? What shall I say to you? Shall I commend you in this? No, I will not.
>
> For I received from the Lord what I also delivered to you, that the Lord Jesus on the night when he was betrayed took bread, and when he had given thanks, he broke it, and said, "This is my body, which is for you. Do this in remembrance of me." In the same way also he took the cup, after supper, saying, "This

cup is the new covenant in my blood. Do this, as often as you drink it, in remembrance of me." For as often as you eat this bread and drink the cup, you proclaim the Lord's death until he comes.

Whoever, therefore, eats the bread or drinks the cup of the Lord in an unworthy manner will be guilty concerning the body and blood of the Lord. Let a person examine himself, then, and so eat of the bread and drink of the cup. For anyone who eats and drinks without discerning the body eats and drinks judgment on himself. That is why many of you are weak and ill, and some have died. But if we judged ourselves truly, we would not be judged. But when we are judged by the Lord, we are disciplined so that we may not be condemned along with the world.

So then, my brothers, when you come together to eat, wait for one another—if anyone is hungry, let him eat at home—so that when you come together it will not be for judgment. About the other things I will give directions when I come. (1 Cor. 11:17–34)

The apostle does not pull any punches here. His words for the Corinthians are hard-hitting. He cannot commend them. In fact, when they gather for the Lord's Supper, "it is not for the better but for the worse" (1 Cor. 11:17). Rather than show up for Communion, they would have done everyone a favor by staying home; their gatherings were a disaster. Then comes the most devastating judgment of all: "When you come together, it is not the Lord's supper that you eat" (v. 20). You might call it "the Lord's Supper," but what you are doing is not a celebration Jesus would recognize. It is something else entirely.

What strong criticism and a stinging rebuke from the apostle! So, *what is going on in Corinth?*

Paul tells us in verse 18 that there are divisions among the people and divisions of a particular kind. Notice what is happening: "For in eating, each one goes ahead with his own meal. One goes hungry, another gets drunk. What! Do you not have houses to eat and drink in? Or do you despise the church of God and humiliate those who have nothing? What shall I say to you? Shall I commend you in this? No, I will not" (vv. 21–22).

To understand what Paul is describing, we need to transport ourselves away from our present context and the way we do Communion with our small cups and tiny pieces of bread or wafer. Instead, we must imagine a community meal such as a church potluck. Evidently, these believers would eat a more substantial meal together when they celebrated the Lord's Supper. Everyone may have brought and eaten their own food, or they all brought something with the idea of sharing it. We cannot really know.

At this point in history, they would not necessarily have had Sunday as a day off work, so they may have gathered at the end of the working day. Perhaps the wealthier members of the congregation did not have to work, but many would have had to (and certainly those who served as slaves). So they may have come to the gathering at the end of a long day, tired and hungry. Some may have showed up later, perhaps as soon as they could get away from work.

And here is what was happening: those who either got there first—or those who could afford to provide food for themselves—were going ahead and having a great feast, and some were even getting drunk on the wine they brought. However, while that was happening in one part of the room or one part of the house, other members of the church who came late from work or who did not have any food to bring were going hungry and being humiliated in the process.

And so, the Lord's Supper, far from being a time for expressing unity as the body of Christ, became a time for drawing attention to some of the deepest divisions in the church. Social and economic divisions were amplified, compounded, and displayed for all to see.

In short, there was a crisis of division at Corinth, division along socioeconomic lines.

Now, we read Paul's text, and I think we are inclined to view this situation as a piece of historical curiosity. *What a shame things were like that at Corinth. How appalling that they let Communion become so divisive.*

Of course, our context is different. We distribute symbolic portions of juice and cracker, so the matter of being hungry or being visibly excluded from a meal is not as relevant here. Moreover, we live in societies with developed social welfare systems, so perhaps we feel the reality of poverty and inequality a little less acutely than other societies in other times and places.

At the same time, I wonder if we are entirely free of the failings and weaknesses Paul identifies at Corinth. Could there be social divisions beneath the surface in our local fellowship? Could there be divisions we might not recognize?

For instance, if you live in a relatively prosperous place, I wonder how easily people settle into the church family if they are struggling a bit more financially.

If you live in a relatively well-educated area, I wonder what it is like for those who never went to college or university, or maybe never finished high school, to settle into your church family. I wonder what it has been like for you, wherever you live and whatever your background may be.

In culturally diverse but still majority white and European-descent communities, I wonder what your experience of becoming part of a church family has been like if you are from another background.

During the outbreak of the coronavirus, I was sobered to hear increased talk of the problem of racism in Canada. I first picked up that concern in the British media before the Canadian Broadcasting Company reported it and was shocked to read this headline in London's newspaper *The Guardian:* "Canada's Chinese community faces racist abuse in wake of coronavirus."[3] That shocked me. *That is not us,* I thought. *That is not Canada.* But where are our blind spots in this even as a church?

Hence, as we consider possible divisions along economic or cultural lines, we may realize that we do gravitate toward those who are most like us and that Paul's lessons for the Corinthians are lessons we need to hear ourselves.

In fact, if we look afresh at the meaning, significance, and proper practice of the Lord's Supper, I believe we will be moved to repent of wrong attitudes. We will be transformed again by the truth of the gospel that makes a different and divided people *one in Christ.*

---

3. Leyland Cecco, "Canada's Chinese Community Faces Racist Abuse in Wake of Coronavirus," *The Guardian* (January 28, 2020), https://www.theguardian.com/world/2020/jan/28/canad-chinese-community-battles-racist-backlash-amid-coronavirus-outbreak.

So, having told us of a crisis at Corinth and having put his finger on what we ourselves need to consider, Paul now issues two prerogatives.

One, he issues a call to remember from Jesus Himself:

> For I received from the Lord what I also delivered to you, that the Lord Jesus on the night when he was betrayed took bread, and when he had given thanks, he broke it, and said, "This is my body, which is for you. Do this in remembrance of me." In the same way also he took the cup, after supper, saying, "This cup is the new covenant in my blood. Do this, as often as you drink it, in remembrance of me." For as often as you eat this bread and drink the cup, you proclaim the Lord's death until he comes. (1 Cor. 11: 23–26)

Jesus declared that the bread represents *His body* and that His disciples should eat it in remembrance of Him. Jesus said that the cup represents the new covenant in *His blood*. As often as we drink it, we remember Him and the shedding of His blood.

Gathering for this special Supper is an occasion, above all else, for *remembrance*.

Now, you may have wonderful recall, or perhaps you are facing memory challenges as you age. I am still relatively young, but my poor memory has become the family joke. I will head upstairs to do a job but reach the top of the stairs and forget entirely why I came up there in the first place. Just yesterday, we were heading out in the car, and I put the indicator on to make a left turn when our destination was to the right. My wife politely asked me where I thought I was going, and I had to admit that I did not have a compelling answer available for her.

Whatever our age, we all have a propensity to forget, and memory aids can be blessings to us. I am thankful my phone pings at me fifteen minutes before every meeting and appointment. I am thankful for ways technology can remind us of birthdays and significant deadlines or tell us when the food is cooked, the furnace filter needs to be changed, or the car needs maintenance.

Memory aids are good, and *visual aids* are even better. Moreover, nowhere do we need more help in remembering than when it comes to the gift of our salvation. We need to be reminded of the foundation of all that we have and are. We need to be reminded and tangibly shown that our invitation to this meal came at great cost. A body had to be *broken* because of my sin; blood had to be *spilled* because of my wrongdoing. The

Son of God gave Himself for me. That is the starting point and foundation for why we observe Communion.

But you and I forget. Consider when we first come to understand that Jesus was betrayed and gave Himself to a gruesome, violent death for us and for our salvation. The gospel message captivates our hearts and calls forth our gratitude, love, and praise. His salvation is fresh in our minds and shapes everything we do. But that memory so often fades.

"Tell Me the Old, Old Story" is a simple hymn that is not sung much now, but I think it captures this dynamic of the forgetful heart. Perhaps you know it:

> *Tell me the old, old story*
> *Of unseen things above,*
> *Of Jesus and His glory,*
> *Of Jesus and His love. . . .*
>
> *Tell me the story slowly,*
> *That I may take it in—*
> *That wonderful redemption,*
> *God's remedy for sin.*
>
> *Tell me the story often,*
> *For I forget so soon;*
> *The early dew of morning*
> *Has passed away at noon.*

Tell me the same old story
When you have cause to fear
That this world's empty glory
Is costing me too dear.

Tell me the old, old story
Of Jesus and His love.[4]

You and I need to hear the story of Jesus and His love for us at Calvary. We need to hear it again and again, and the Lord knows *we need to see it* as well. He has given us His Supper as a reminder and a tangible visual aid of the gospel.

The Lord's Supper is a powerful occasion of remembrance for us all. At this Table, everything else is stripped away. We may be rich or poor, rejoicing or mourning, riding high on a wave of triumph or wading in a sea of despair, but at this Table we are one thing and one thing only: sinners redeemed by the blood of the Lamb, guilty people justified by the broken body of the Son of God. We are children of the King bought at a tremendous cost. That is who we are at this Table.

And if we have forgotten—if, as the hymn writer says, "the early dew of morning has passed away at noon," if "this world's empty glory is costing [us] too dear"[5] because we have been swept up in it—here is our reset, our reminder, our

---

4. Kate Hankey, "Tell Me the Old, Old Story," public domain.
5. Hankey, "Tell Me the Old, Old Story."

recalibration of the heart. Communion is a call to remember from Jesus Himself.

I am no great musician, but I enjoy playing the piano and have always loved playing an acoustic piano whenever I have the opportunity. We recently acquired an old piano in our house that was made in the 1920s in Germany. It comes from another time and another world. As it happens, the lady from whom we bought it said it had been in her family for nearly seventy years, and she had brought it over to Canada from Europe.

When we had the piano tuned, the tuner told us to expect that, over the course of the winter, the tuning in this old piano would change as the atmosphere and humidity in the house changes. Then we would need to tune it again in the spring, and probably in the autumn, to get it back to accurate pitch.

As I look at the strings and the soundboard of this old piano, it seems to me to illustrate something of my heart. You see, our hearts slide out of tune. They forget the accurate pitch of the gospel. They need to be retuned and recalibrated, and they need it regularly. And the Lord's Supper is given to us to enable that to happen.

The idea of joining in a meal together is a powerful symbol with profound meaning in Scripture. When God's people eat a meal together, it means something. In fact, the meal Jesus was eating with His disciples was itself a reminder of a famous meal earlier in biblical history.

When the Israelites were liberated from slavery in Egypt, they were instructed to take a lamb and kill it and put the blood on the doorframes of their homes. When the angel of death came over the land of Egypt, it would "pass over" the homes of the Israelites and bring no destruction to them. The Israelites then ate the lamb with unleavened bread, before departing Egypt in something of a hurry. Thus, that Passover meal was to be celebrated every year because it was a reminder of the salvation and liberation God had achieved for them. And it was that meal Jesus and His disciples were having together on the night He was betrayed.

The Passover meal was a great reminder of God's covenant commitment to His people, a reminder of that defining act of salvation.

So, when we gather around the Lord's Table, we remember the Lord's covenant commitment to us in Christ. We remember God's great saving act when He freed us from sin and destruction through the shed blood of the Lamb.

Passover is a milestone meal from salvation history, but it also points us forward to another great meal yet to come: "For as often as you eat this bread and drink this cup, *you proclaim the Lord's death until he comes*" (11: 26, emphasis added).

We look forward to the fact that our crucified, risen, and ascended Lord is going to come back for us. And when He gathers His people, in a day yet to come, we are told there will be a great banquet. John writes in Revelation 19:6–9 of "the marriage supper of the Lamb." On a coming day, the Lamb of God will gather His people to Himself for a feast—a wedding banquet—when the Lamb will take to Himself the church He bought at such great cost.

And so, as we gather around this Table as the saved people of God, we remember our rescue and proclaim to the world that we await the Lamb's return. As we gather, we anticipate the day we will sit at His Table in glory.

The Lord's Supper is our great memory aid, our powerful *visual aid* of the gospel. The elements of the bread and the cup are not magical, but rather, are just ordinary food. Eating and drinking does not take away our sin or make us more holy. Rather, the elements remind us that we come to God, and we come together because of a gruesome act of violence, an act of extraordinary sacrifice.

And so, at the Table, there is a call to remember Jesus.

Two, at the Lord's Supper, there is a call to examine ourselves. Because we are remembering such momentous and sacred events, we need to approach the Table carefully: "Whoever, therefore, eats the bread or drinks the cup of the Lord in an unworthy manner will be guilty concerning the body and blood of the Lord. Let a person examine himself, then, and so eat of the bread and drink of the cup" (vv. 27–28).

Paul wants us to see that, when we remember the Lord's death, there is a kind of behavior and attitude that is worthy of the occasion, and a kind that is unworthy. But what precisely does he have in mind? Verse 29 says that the *unworthy* thing to do is to eat and drink without discerning "the body."

But that raises another question: What "body" is Paul referring to? He may be referring to the broken body of Jesus; that is, if we eat and drink unreflectively and without remembering Jesus's broken body, that brings judgment. That is one possibility. But the more likely possibility is that Paul is referring to the *body of believers* who make up His church.

Paul has spoken of the church as "the body" already in his letter, and if you look ahead to chapter 12 and verse 12, you see that he is going to spend much of this next chapter talking about how Christians are all part of the one "body" of Christ.

That fits well with where Paul began. Remember that he was concerned that the Corinthians were not treating one another well or behaving as a true body of believers. To eat and drink without discerning the body would be to eat and drink and completely fail to see or care for the body of Christ all around us—the people of Christ who make up His church.

That is just what was happening at Corinth. The result was sobering. The Lord brought a serious discipline upon the church for their sin: "That is why many of you are weak and ill, and some have died" (11:30).

Unsurprisingly, Paul goes on to tell them to sort out the situation quickly. He says in verse 33: "So then, my brothers, when you come together to eat, wait for one another." Show one another proper care and loving concern and do so in order that your gatherings might be healthy and not destructive. Do so in order that it might truly be the Lord's Supper you eat.

The Lord's Supper is meant to be an occasion when the unity of the church is symbolized and expressed. There is something powerful in sharing a meal together. That is true in any context: a big family dinner when everyone takes time to gather; a married couple who has a chance to go out to supper on a Friday night; a business meeting, when sitting down over lunch often makes the crucial difference in finalizing an agreement.

For the church, gathering around this Table is a powerful symbol of our unity. Paul points us in that direction back in chapter 10, where he says that "because there is one bread, we who are many are one body, for we all partake of the one bread" (v. 17).

The Lord's Supper reminds us of our unity in Christ and allows us to express that unity in a tangible way. But at the same time, Paul warns us that when the reality on the ground denies the symbol, it is possible that members of the church could be eating and drinking judgment on themselves as they gather at the Table.

This call, this admonition, to examine ourselves because we can face judgment or *discipline* for approaching the Lord's Supper wrongly is a serious call. Gathering at the Lord's Table is a spiritually significant time of meeting with the Lord and of fellowship with one another. This admonition tells us that if we presume to take part in this symbol while at the same time engaging in persistent and deliberate sin, we are doing something dangerous and even inviting the Lord's discipline.

You sometimes hear these horror stories of unhappy and dysfunctional families coming together for feasts at Thanksgiving or Christmas or anniversaries. Everyone dreads the gathering and harbors hatred, hurt, unresolved conflict, and bitterness. It is a hornet's nest of misery and anger. But everyone dresses up and smiles as best as they can; they get through the meal and leave as promptly as possible. We all know the stories. Maybe you have experienced something like that yourself.

Likewise, a church can be so filled with discourtesy and disagreement that the gatherings of the Lord's Supper could look the same: a veneer of fellowship that masks discord.

The warning here for the Corinthians is recorded for us with good reason. The call to examine ourselves is a call for you and me. As we gather, we must examine ourselves and ask: "Is my heart shaped by a remembrance of the sacrifice of Jesus? Am I discerning the body of Christ, the people of Christ, around me in this fellowship? Am I honoring Jesus by honoring them? Does my life reflect the reality of this fellowship with Jesus and fellowship with His people? Or is there a disconnect? Have I been discourteous or unloving to the people who are part of the body of Christ with me? Do I have an attitude of heart that is wrong?"

Perhaps as we reflect and examine ourselves, we see in our heart an attitude that is unworthy, a sin that has not been addressed. Perhaps as we gather at the Table, we are prompted to confess the sin in our heart to the Lord and to turn from it. Perhaps we are prompted to go and make something right with a brother or sister in Christ.

As we consider verses 28 and 29, I think it is possible to respond wrongly in two ways. One way is to harden our hearts and ignore the admonition here, to gloss it over and assume it does not apply to us. The second way is to take it to heart so much that we begin to think we could never come to the Lord's Table because, each time we examine ourselves, we find sin in our heart and evidence of sin in our lives. We think to ourselves: *I am not worthy. I cannot be worthy; I can never approach the Table of the Lord.*

Considering this danger, the French Reformer John Calvin once wrote:

Therefore, this is the worthiness—the best and only kind we can bring to God—to offer our vileness and (so to speak) our unworthiness to him so that his mercy may make us worthy of him; to despair in ourselves so that we may be comforted in him; to abase ourselves so that we may be lifted up by him; to accuse ourselves so that we may be justified by him.[6]

Calvin's words are helpful here. We come to the Table to remember that we are unworthy in ourselves and that the Son of God had to shed His blood and give His body to be broken so we could be made worthy. We gather to remember that He was condemned that we might be justified. And so we come on the basis of His work at Calvary and His work alone.

As we gather at the Table, we heed Christ's call to remember and to examine ourselves. When we do so, our gatherings take on a new significance. We move beyond tradition and reflex to something deeper and more meaningful that will impact our life together as the family of God. The reminder of His death and of our unity together in Christ becomes everything to us. And the result is that we grow in our love for Jesus and for one another.

---

6. John Calvin, *Institutes of the Christian Religion*, 4.17.42, The Library of Christian Classics, vol. 21, John T. McNeill, ed., Ford Lewis Battles, trans. (Philadelphia: Westminster, 1960).

If that happens, by the grace of God, so much else that is good and healthy will flow from it. Our church life, our ministry, and our impact will be transformed. This is the reason the Lord has called us to gather at His Table to remember and to examine our hearts.

6

• • • • • • •

Gathered to Invest

WHAT DO I REALLY TREASURE IN THIS LIFE? WHAT AM I
investing in? Where are the affections of my heart set? These
are challenging questions for us to consider.

Jesus observes in His Sermon on the Mount: "Where your
treasure is, there your heart will be also" (Matt. 6:21). Here He
issues a challenge in terms we can understand and quantify; He
is speaking of financial and material gain.

In "Gathered to Give," we looked at three key principles
about Christian giving the apostle Paul sets out in 2 Corinthians
8 and 9. Namely, our giving is shaped by grace, marked by generosity, and is for God's glory. God has gathered us as His people
by His grace. Our financial giving will be the work of God in

and through us, says Scripture. As we give, we are instruments of God Himself to extend His grace to others.

Now in Matthew 6, Jesus frames the challenge and the question as a matter of *investing*: namely, choosing and finding the right asset in which to place our resources.

The financial marketplace can be a bewildering place with so many investment options to choose from: stocks, bonds, mutual funds, ETFs, REITs, hedge funds, and the list goes on. Selecting investments can be overwhelming for even the most financially literate to navigate.

But Jesus sets basic asset classes before us as two places to invest. He says we must choose between investing in *earthly treasure* and *heavenly treasure*. That is it, plain and simple. And, unsurprisingly, Jesus's simple agenda in this passage is to persuade us to invest in the latter rather than the former.

So let us look at three investment principles Jesus offers us in Matthew 6.

One, invest in heavenly treasure because it is lasting. Jesus urges us, "Do not lay up for yourselves treasures on earth, where moth and rust destroy and where thieves break in and steal, but lay up for yourselves treasures in heaven, where neither moth nor rust destroys and where thieves do not break in and steal" (vv. 19–20).

I liked cars when I was a child, and so my father would take me to the big automotive exhibition in Toronto to see all the latest models. Some of those cars looked so wonderful then; they were shiny luxury brands and exciting sports cars.

I still see some of those models on the road that I remember seeing as a child when they were new. But here is the funny thing: unless someone has taken amazing care of them, they look like real rust buckets now! I imagine you would have to pay to have someone scrap them for you.

Of course, in Canada where I live, we have salty winter roads. I saw the first little rust patch on our car not so long ago, and when you see that, you know it is the beginning of the end—it is only a matter of time. Try as you may, you cannot keep the salt off them. We went to the car wash yesterday and then drove on to our next stop. But by the time we got out of the car only ten minutes later, it was totally spattered with salt as if it had never been washed. Fighting rust is a losing battle.

Fighting moths is similar. When we lived in London some years ago, a plague of moths invaded the city, and the old Victorian houses were hit hard. We moved into one such house and quickly began to notice little holes appearing in our sweaters, jackets, and just about anything made of natural fiber. By the time we left, few garments had escaped unscathed.

This is a world, Jesus reminds us, where moth and rust destroy. It is also a world where thieves break in and steal.

Ottawa is hardly a crime-ridden city, but we had a spate of automobile thefts not long ago. The police broke a major car-theft ring and recovered ninety-seven vehicles. One woman even reported her second car had been stolen in eighteen months. Her insurance company replaced her first stolen car, but then one morning she looked out the window to discover that her brand-new replacement car had now been stolen right off her driveway.

Do not lay up for yourselves treasures on earth, where moth and rust destroy and where thieves break in and steal.

It is a bad investment, says Jesus, to store up treasures on earth. This earth is not a sensible place to put your resources if you want them to last.

Recently, Parks Canada released images of artifacts from the doomed 1840s Franklin expedition to the Arctic Ocean. One featured a hairbrush recovered from the sunken ship. Most of the bristles were gone, but you could still recognize a hairbrush. It is amazing to see what remains after nearly two centuries at the bottom of the Arctic. Nevertheless, the image is a stark reminder of how this is a world of decay.

This world is no safe haven for our treasure, Jesus reminds us. But one place is truly safe, and one repository for wealth is entirely secure. No, it is not the vault of a Swiss bank or Fort Knox or the Tower of London. It is heaven itself: "Lay up for yourselves treasures in heaven, where neither moth nor rust destroys and where thieves do not break in and steal" (v. 20).

Heaven is where to invest. In principle, we may understand this. But what about the mechanics, the practicalities?

We can easily move money around different accounts these days. If you want to put money into savings, just open your app. If you want to send money to a family member or friend, just do a quick e-transfer.

But how do we invest in heaven? What will it look like, in practical terms, to pivot away from investing in the things of this world and, instead, to invest in heaven?

To answer that question, we must think about heavenly riches. Specifically, what things—what riches—go beyond this life and into the life to come?

Presumably our own character and relationship with the Lord are part of this answer. When we invest in knowing Him more, loving Him more, and becoming more Christlike with the help of the Holy Spirit, we trust that a deepening relationship with the Lord and a growing godliness will go with us into His presence in the life to come. So investments in godliness, Christlikeness, our walk with the Lord, and our knowledge of His Word are lasting investments for each one of us.

Added to that, we can take *other people* with us to heaven too. We cannot take possessions, but we can take men and women and boys and girls who hear the gospel and respond in repentance and faith. Other people—*other saved people*—are heavenly riches. Their eternal souls are lasting investments.

Now bring these insights back into the realm of investing. You and I have the opportunity to spend our lives either investing in *things,* worldly possessions, or in *heavenly riches*—growing in love and knowledge of the Lord and helping other people know Him and love Him too. And we get to choose how we invest.

It is an either-or choice, according to Jesus. When we consider that, we see how our choice here will impact all of life.

Our choice will impact our use of the funds in our bank account, to be sure. We can either spend our money on ourselves, or we can make sacrificial decisions to give a portion of those funds away regularly to the work of the gospel. That is an obvious way to invest.

At the same time, Matthew 6 applies to much more than the money in our bank account. Yes, our finances are the first and most obvious line of application, but the challenge of Jesus extends more broadly to the choices we make about *how* we use the things we have.

For example, for most of us, our homes are our most valuable possession. When it comes to using our homes, we can either think of them as our personal palaces to enjoy and to seek refuge from the world, or we can think of our homes as ministry tools to use for the kingdom and for investing in heavenly riches. We can think of them as strategic places of hospitality where we can welcome brothers and sisters in Christ who need encouragement in the faith and help to grow, where we can disciple others, formally and informally. We can use our homes strategically, as gospel outposts in our neighborhoods, where friends and neighbors can be welcomed, can experience Christian hospitality, and perhaps can hear the gospel.

It is a decision about how we invest.

But Jesus's challenge goes further yet and runs deeper still. Indeed, our choice impacts what we do with *our whole life*: what job we do, what dreams we pursue, and what projects and priorities we give ourselves to. Ultimately, these things are all about *investing*. We have one life to live. What are we doing with it? How are we spending it?

We each need to consider that challenge carefully. In our comfortable Western context, we are all inclined to follow the local religion of pursuing the middle-class dream as our main priority: get a good education, land a steady job, buy a good home, retire as early as we can, and just be *comfortable*. In many ways, this is our default. And so, our Christianity becomes kind of an add-on that we add on top or fit around this main thing we are doing—this *core priority of making ourselves comfortable and secure.*

In verses 19 and 20, Jesus is challenging us to something different. He is challenging us to spend our life resources investing in a heavenly future, not an earthly one.

If we are thinking of accumulating the earthly treasure of wealth or status or fame or success, we plan our lives around those things by pursuing the education and the career path that will maximize earthly treasure. In our work, we will climb as high as we can, as fast as we can. We grow the business as big as it can get and give the job all the hours we have just like everyone else.

But if we are thinking about heavenly treasure, we might do the same job and pursue the same career path, but we might say: "You know what, maybe I will decline the promotion. Maybe I will limit the hours a bit. I am going to keep the company a little smaller on purpose so that I have the time to invest in heavenly treasure, so that I have the time to teach my kids the Word of God and shepherd them at home. I am going to do this so that I have time to get to know my neighbors and colleagues so that perhaps I can be a witness to them in some way, and so that I have time to serve at church as an elder or teaching Sunday school or working in the outreach ministry. I want time to invest in those things because that is an investment in lasting treasure. Sure, it will limit my professional reputation and may limit my income. But it is a strategic investment choice and a sound one."

We have been considering what gathering looks like within our local church family. God calls us to invest deeply by meeting together on Sundays, committing to the responsibilities of membership, giving, serving, and more. But each of us will only have the capacity to do those things *corporately* if our values are set in the right place *personally*. We can only do this if we have structured our lives so that we have capacity, space, and availability to be involved in church life in that way. We should be treasuring Christ individually if we are going to be able to treasure Him together.

Perhaps you are at a stage of life when you are thinking through the future, what you will study and what job you will pursue. You are asking the big questions: "What am I going to invest myself in? What am I going to spend this one life doing?" All around you, people will be investing in earthly treasure, one way or another. But the call on your life, if you belong to Jesus Christ, is this: whatever you study, whatever you do for a living, invest your time, energies, and gifts in heavenly treasure.

For some, that will mean doing normal jobs but prayerfully and carefully prioritizing God's kingdom in various ways as you work. For others, this will mean thinking about full-time ministry of some kind such as training to be a pastor, a missionary, or another vocational gospel worker.

At the church where I pastor, we have a tremendous legacy of a missions program with missionary partners around the world. Our dream is to develop it further and expand its reach. But the basic reality is that our missions program will only grow if people (especially young people) from our church family will stand up and say: "I want to invest my life in heavenly treasure, winning the souls who will join me in heaven. I want to go where the Lord would send me." We recognize that our missions program will inevitably wither and die if we do not see a new generation of missionaries coming forward, ready to invest and ready to serve.

I know that many young people may dismiss that idea and discount the possibility of vocational Christian ministry. From what I have seen, there will be two main reasons. These are not the only reasons, but they are significant. First is the desire to make more money in secular employment. Second is the preference of parents (and often Christian parents) that their children pursue more prestigious, stable, and lucrative careers.

I have seen this time and again; often for young people seriously considering costly, sacrificial service of Jesus Christ, the greatest dissuaders will be parents who dislike the idea of its cost. They would rather see their children be more comfortable.

I say this because I want to encourage those of us who are parents to put our convictions into practice when it comes to our children. I want us to encourage our children to invest in heavenly treasure. We might be willing to make that investment ourselves in costly ways, but when it comes to our children and their worldly comfort and prosperity, suddenly we forget our convictions, and we become more worldly in our thinking. I can see how I might do that, and I can imagine how you might too. But if we take Jesus seriously, we will want to do everything we can to encourage our children to pursue heavenly treasure in a wholehearted way. After all, it makes sense. It is a good investment. It is the best way to use the gifts and opportunities afforded us in this one life God has given us.

Invest in heavenly treasure because it is lasting.

Two, invest in heavenly treasure because your heart will follow. Do not lay up treasure on earth, but lay it up in heaven, Jesus urges us. Notice what He says next in Matthew 6:21: "For where your treasure is, there your heart will be also."

Here Jesus shows us once again His deep insight into the way the human heart works.

If I were writing verses 19 to 21, here is what I would say: "Look, you need to be investing in the right things—not in perishable earthly things but in heavenly things. So here is my advice: start with your heart—check your motivations and your value system. If you get your motivations and your value system right over time through prayer, study, and growing maturity, then you will find that you naturally start to invest in the right things and not the wrong things. Get your heart right, and then your behavior will naturally follow."

Makes sense, right? The appropriate way to bring about lasting change in behavior is to start with the heart. But Jesus does not say that here; that is not His approach. Instead, He begins in verse 19 with a direct focus on the behavior. He starts with the behavior and not the heart.

He tells us to take practical steps to make the investment in heavenly treasure. Rather than buying the next toy or luxury, use the money instead for supporting gospel work. Do something practical here: write a check, make an investment in the kingdom (vv. 19–20), *"for* where your treasure is, there your heart will be also" (v. 21, emphasis added).

That is, if you take the money and buy the toy, your heart will follow, and you will love that thing. That is what happens; we love the things we put our money into. For instance, you are searching the market for a new house. Options are limited, and you are not quite sure, but you buy the one with the questionable green carpet or dated wood-paneled walls because you recognize it is the best option. You hand over the down payment and then start slogging away, making the monthly mortgage payments. And as you invest, what happens? Your affection for the house grows. It is yours, and you are investing in it. You see a future for it. The house becomes home. Your heart follows your money.

Jesus says to us, as a matter of wisdom and obedience, *invest in heavenly things.* Take the money that might go on a toy and put it into a gospel priority, a gospel project where there will be eternal fruit, and your heart will follow. You will think, *I put hard-earned cash into this, and it matters to me that it succeeds. I have a stake in it.* You follow the project, you pray for the work, and suddenly, you find that you care more deeply about the eternal impact of this endeavor. Your heart is lifted up to heavenly things as you invest earthly resources into them.

So what Jesus is saying is this: *your wallet has the capacity to teach your heart a lesson.* Your checkbook has the power to redirect your affections. Your banking app can shape what you love most.

Jesus's teaching is the reverse of what we might assume. It sounds so pragmatic, so functional. But it is the wisdom of Jesus. He knows what we are like. He knows that our heart will follow the money.

That insight tells us something important about our own discipleship. It tells us that, if we find our heart is not set on heavenly things—if we find that we are too much in love with this present world and with pursuing the things of this world—the effective way to change our heart and redirect our affections is to make some practical treasure decisions. Invest money in the kingdom. Make the decision to start putting a tithe, 10 percent of income, into gospel work. Make the decision to reduce your hours at work and invest the time in some form of ministry. Make the decision to invest a week in the summer in a short-term missions trip. Take some practical steps to redirect your resources—time, money, energy, gifts—away from earthy investments and into heavenly investments. And just see what happens to your heart and your affections.

Now verses 22 and 23 of Matthew 6 are often viewed as some of the most perplexing words from Jesus. They are not easy to interpret, but as far as I can tell, He is reinforcing this same point here. Jesus says: "The eye is the lamp of the body. So, if your eye is healthy, your whole body will be full of light, but if your eye is bad, your whole body will be full of darkness. If then the light in you is darkness, how great is the darkness!"

Where we point our eyes and fix our gaze significantly impacts our inner life and heart. If we fix our eyes on things that are dark and of little worth (the things of this world) rather than the things of heaven, our heart will live in the shadows. But if we take practical steps to turn our eyes to the light, to bright things and to heaven above, that light will enter deep within through those two lamps of the body, and our whole inner life will be filled with light.

Imagine a submarine where the crew inside can only look through the periscope to see the world around them. Where they point the periscope drastically affects all they see from within that tube below the waves. The periscope is powerful and influential within that submarine. It is the only window on the world and gives shape to everything else.

The point is this: take practical steps to turn your eyes to things of true value. Turn to the light. Or, to go back to the practical language of verse 21, use your "treasure" to turn your attention to the right place, and your "heart"—your inner life—will follow.

Invest in heavenly treasure because it will direct your heart. *Three, invest in heavenly treasure because you can only serve one master.* Jesus says in verse 24: "No one can serve two masters, for either he will hate the one and love the other, or he will be devoted to the one and despise the other. You cannot serve God and money."

We are creatures that prefer not to choose. We like to have it both ways. We like to be able to play at work and often insist on bringing work into our play. I read of the rising trend of people taking vacation days from work to have free time to catch up on their *work*. I remember reading a survey once that found 16 percent of American workers take time off work to do more work. At the same time, a major bank in the United Kingdom courted controversy by introducing software to spy on their employees to make sure they were actually working when they were at work and not away from their desks chatting or lost in the world of social media while staring at the screen.

While visiting a local restaurant, I came across the new phenomenon of blending two courses in one dish. Maybe you have seen this. We modern and sophisticated people do not want to have to choose between an entrée and a dessert; we want both at once. To meet that desire, this restaurant now offers hamburgers with chocolate-filled beef patties and a range of dessert toppings to adorn the burger alongside the ketchup. I can hardly think of anything more unappealing myself, but evidently there is a market.

We struggle to choose one thing or another, and we certainly do not like to be constrained. But Jesus wants us to know that in this most significant matter we absolutely must make a choice. We must choose whether we will serve *God or money*. We would love to think we can do both. I fear that in our wealthy context we have kidded ourselves far too often into thinking we can serve both God and money effectively. But Jesus says we cannot.

The reason we cannot serve both is because both demand to be our master. Both demand to have our all. The reality is that we will give ourselves fully to one or the other, but we do not have the capacity to love and serve both at the same time.

In fact, the language of "service" here in verse 24 could equally be translated in terms of "slavery." No one can be a slave of two masters. We are owned by one or the other.

God will not tolerate us giving our heart to money, and money will not give way to God if we allow it free reign in our affections.

When Jesus puts the matter in such stark terms, we realize He is calling us to choose who or what, ultimately, will be our God. Will we serve and worship the true and living God, or will we serve and worship the false god, the idol of money and material wealth?

We might try to dismiss this sharp distinction as radical and extreme. We might try to protest that we can hold on to a flirtation with money but keep God at the true center of our affections. But I think we all know in our heart of hearts that money, possessions, and wealth have this tendency to demand more and more of us.

John D. Rockefeller's reported quip about money is so accurate. As the story is often told, when he was the richest man on earth, he was asked how much money was enough. His answer was as simple as it was quick: "Just a little bit more."

How accurate. Earthly treasure is a cruel master because it always wants more of us; it always demands more. And the danger is that it will quickly displace the Lord Himself from His rightful place in our heart.

You may know the name of C. T. Studd. He was a famous British missionary to China, India, and Africa a century ago. He was born into a wealthy and privileged English family and benefited from a fine education. He made his name early in the world of cricket, playing for England against Australia in 1882.

But when he came to Christ, he began to reevaluate what truly mattered in this life. He was confronted with the question, "What is all the fame and flattery worth . . . when a man comes to face eternity?" And he concluded, in his own words: "I know that cricket would not last, and honour would not last, and nothing in this world would last, but it was worthwhile living for the world to come."

Studd left the comforts of wealth in England, gave away his substantial inheritance to the work of the gospel, and labored to bring the good news to people who had not heard. He is perhaps best remembered for his famous poem, which sums up so well the message of Matthew 6: "Only one life, 'twill soon be passed, only what's done for Christ will last."

Friend, where are you investing today? Where is your treasure? Where is heart? Who is your Master and your God?

7

. . . .

Gathered to Pray

ONE OF THE GREAT DANGERS FOR US AS A PEOPLE OF GOD gathered as a fellowship is that we can be energetic doers but rather reluctant "pray-ers." If we are zealous for the Lord, committed to the work of ministry, eager to see the gospel go forth, we can apply ourselves energetically to the opportunities before us while giving little thought or time to the privilege of prayer.

On a personal level, I think that most of us (if we are honest) find prayer a little difficult. Perhaps the easiest way to embarrass Christians is to ask them about the state of their prayer life. Most of us are not as prayerful as we would like to be or sense we ought to be. When we are in crisis and have a particular need before us, we will be moved to pray with urgency, but even unbelievers will sometimes do that. Nothing is remarkable about praying in a crisis. But in the day-to-day rhythms of life, we find it hard.

You may have noticed that when a church has a prayer gathering, only a small fraction of the Sunday congregation will generally attend. The traditional midweek prayer service has largely been displaced by the small-group Bible study in many churches. Yet often in a small-group gathering, after coffee, catch-up, and perhaps a study, time is squeezed for prayer, or prayer is skipped altogether.

We can be active as local fellowships; our ministry calendars can be filled with many people engaged in good activities. *But what about prayer?* Is your congregation a praying church? Are we a people marked and characterized by prayer?

These are challenging questions to face, and they lead us naturally to consider another question: How does God's Word direct us when it comes to prayer and the family of God? I think we know the answer in some ways: we should be prayerful; we ought to prioritize prayer. Prayer is a good and right thing to do. We understand that. But let us then sharpen the inquiry a little more: *Why?* Why should we be a praying family?

From Scripture, I want to highlight four factors that should drive us to be a praying church family. I am sure there are more, but let us focus on these four.

One, we are to be a praying family because of the Father's invitation. This is the simplest and most obvious factor to observe about prayer in the Bible. God wants us to pray. He invites us to pray, and He calls us to pray.

We see this invitation to pray immediately when we read the various epistles addressed to the whole church. Notice what Paul writes in 1 Thessalonians 5:15–22:

> See that no one repays anyone evil for evil, but always seek to do good to one another and to everyone. Rejoice always, *pray without ceasing, give thanks in all circumstances; for this is the will of God in Christ Jesus for you.* Do not quench the Spirit. Do not despise prophecies, but test everything; hold fast what is good. Abstain from every form of evil. (emphasis added)

Paul is outlining the dynamics of community life in Christ, and what does he say? "Rejoice always, pray without ceasing, give thanks in all circumstances; for this is the will of God in Christ Jesus for you" (vv. 16–18). He communicates a series of basic instructions for the church; at the heart of those is the encouragement to "pray without ceasing, . . . for this is the will of God . . . for you" (vv. 17–18).

We often ask why prayer matters if God is sovereign, knows the future, and is in charge. Why should we be a praying people and a praying church? Here it is. Here is the fundamental answer: because "this is the will of God in Christ Jesus for you." That may not be the complete answer we crave. It may not satisfy all our curiosity about how and why prayer works. *But it is a sufficient answer.* We pray because God has called us to pray, because it is the will of God for us.

This message is reinforced and repeated elsewhere; for instance, in 1 Timothy 2. Here Paul sets out priorities for the church in Ephesus which Timothy was leading. As he sets out priorities and instructions for the church, this one tops the list:

> First of all, then, I urge that supplications, prayers, intercessions, and thanksgivings be made for all people, for kings and all who are in high positions, that we may lead a peaceful and quiet life, godly and dignified in every way. This is good, and it is pleasing in the sight of God our Savior. (vv. 1–3)

"First of all, I urge that you pray," and here is why: "This is good, and it is pleasing in the sight of God our Savior" (v. 3).

God instructs us to do it, and *it pleases Him.* For us who know and love Him, that is reason enough. Do we fully understand all the dynamics of prayer—how it works, why it works, why God has ordained it, and what it achieves? No, we do not. But we know that God has called us to be a people of prayer, and we know that it pleases Him. And that is enough for us as His children.

When we stop to think about it, prayer is the greatest privilege we enjoy in this life. Through prayer, we have access to the throne room of heaven itself.

We know the frustrating experience of trying to arrange a meeting with someone important or to get someone on the phone who is in a position to help us, and yet we get nowhere. I tried to call the passport office recently, and after endless messages, numeric options, and pressing buttons, I was finally told that no one was available to speak to me, and the line went dead. I was not all that surprised; it would have been more surprising to get a person on the line.

On a few occasions when I have been particularly frustrated in dealing with a company, I have called the receptionist and asked to speak with the boss, president, or CEO, but that generally does not work. Usually, the receptionist has been trained never to put the call through, but rather to offer politely to pass on the message.

I remember stopping by the constituency office of my local member of Parliament and asking when it might be possible to have a face-to-face meeting. His kindly office manager gave me a genuinely perplexed look. He had no idea when the MP would be in the constituency office or when we might see him in the neighborhood again. I left my number, but I did not depart holding my breath.

This is just reality, right? It is difficult to get through. The more important the person, the more in demand they are, the smaller our chances of gaining access.

But here is the remarkable reality for the Christian: in prayer, you and I have access to heaven's throne room, the place of supreme power. We have a direct line to the CEO of the universe, the Sovereign of all.

This is a wonderful privilege, and we must remember specifically that this is a *gospel privilege*. God has taken extraordinary steps to make it possible for us to have this access. It is not something we should rightly have. We do not deserve to have the ear of the Almighty. We do not deserve to have access to His presence.

We only have this access as His people because Jesus, our great High Priest, has given Himself to be the sacrifice to pay the price for our sin and to cleanse and forgive us. We only have access because He has risen from the dead and ascended on high to be our intermediary and ever-living Priest. And He invites us to come, to approach, and to pray. Through Him, *the Lord has made it possible.*

Hebrews 4:14–16 says:

> Since then we have a great high priest who has passed through the heavens, Jesus, the Son of

God, let us hold fast our confession. For we do not have a high priest who is unable to sympathize with our weaknesses, but one who in every respect has been tempted as we are, yet without sin. Let us then with confidence draw near to the throne of grace, that we may receive mercy and find grace to help in time of need.

The Lord Jesus Christ came down from heaven and lived among us. He knows the realities of trial and testing. He knows what it is to live life in this world as a human being. Moreover, He went to the cross to pay the price of our sin, and He rose again and ascended on high that He might open the way to give us access to the Father. To all of us who know Him by faith and trust Him, we have been given access to God.

This is our great family privilege. Access to God is the greatest privilege we can know this side of heaven. The privilege is ours and has been made possible through the gospel, but we must make use of it. We ought to be a praying family because of the Father's invitation.

Two, we should be a praying family because of the Father's kindness. In prayer, we so often think of our needs, what we want to ask God to do for us and to provide for us. Our needs are certainly a large part of prayer. But before we get to our needs and requests, more fundamentally, we have so much for which to give thanks to God.

Learning to give thanks is part of growing up. It is a mark of maturity. Small children simply receive what their parents give them. But eventually they learn—we hope—to say, "Thank you." We are touched when a child learns to say thank you and makes a habit of saying it.

Sadly, the art of the thank-you letter is falling out of fashion. In generations gone by, children might have been taught to sit down and write a thank-you letter for a gift received at a birthday or Christmas. We are not so disciplined with that in our generation. But it is right to give thanks when we have been the beneficiaries of kindness.

We have indeed been beneficiaries of the Lord's kindness. We have so much to thank Him for daily. He has made us and given us life. He has provided a bountiful world for us to live in and given us our daily bread. He has poured out His grace and mercy upon us in Christ. He has redeemed us, made us his own, and given His own Son for our salvation. He has opened heaven to us and made us His children. And it is a mark of spiritual life and spiritual maturity to learn to give thanks to Him.

Jesus once met ten lepers on his way to Jerusalem, an event recounted for us in Luke 17. The lepers pleaded with Him for mercy, and He sent them to the priests. On their way, they were healed. One of the ten, when he saw that Jesus had healed him, turned back and praised God. Luke 17:16 says that this man "fell on his face at Jesus' feet, giving him thanks." Jesus then responded, "Were not ten cleansed? Where are the nine? Was no one found to return and give praise to God except this foreigner?" (vv. 17–18).

Where are the nine? We live in a world of entitlement and ingratitude. So often little thanks is offered for anything. So often there is little courtesy, little acknowledgment. But as children of God, we are called to be different. The Lord has poured out His kindness upon us, kindness we could never earn or deserve. And so, as a church family, we must be marked by gratitude that is expressed and poured out in prayer.

"Where are the nine?" asks Jesus. I fear, too often, He might ask where you and I are when it comes to giving Him thanks for His mercies, which overflow so abundantly in our lives and in our churches. Are we driven to our knees to thank Him with hearts full of praise?

We are to be a praying family because of the Lord's kindness.

Three, we are to be a praying family because of the Lord's enabling. Jesus Christ sends His church into the world to spread His word, make disciples, and build up the saints. We are called to speak life to dead people who do not naturally have an interest in hearing. We are called to encourage one another to grow in Christ and serve Him, and it is an uphill battle in every life. We face the constant reality of spiritual opposition from the enemies of God.

And so, we have to recognize and remember that we do not have the resources for this work in and of ourselves. Living the Christian life and engaging in the work of ministry is something that is fundamentally spiritual in nature; we might even say it is supernatural. These things are beyond our natural capacity. They are only possible and doable through the enabling help of God by His Spirit.

Paul urges us:

> Finally, be strong in the Lord and in the strength of his might. Put on the whole armor of God, that you may be able to stand against the schemes of the devil. For we do not wrestle against flesh and blood, but against the rulers, against the authorities, against the cosmic powers over this present darkness, against the spiritual forces of evil in the heavenly places. Therefore take up the whole armor of God, that you may be able to withstand in the evil day, and having done all, to stand firm. . . . *praying at all times in the Spirit, with all prayer and supplication.* To that end, keep alert with all perseverance, making supplication for all the saints, and also for me, that words may be given to me in opening my mouth boldly to proclaim the mystery of the gospel, for which I

am an ambassador in chains, that I may declare
it boldly, as I ought to speak. (Eph 6:10–13,
18–20, emphasis added)

Friend, we must remember that we are engaged in a spiritual battle. The stakes are high, and the resources needed far outstretch our natural abilities. Do not be strong in yourself personally. Let us not be strong in ourselves corporately or in our church size or history or reputation or earthly resources. No, be strong in the Lord and in His might, praying at all times in the Spirit, with all prayer and supplication. We are a praying family because of the Lord's enabling.

Prayerlessness is a kind of functional materialism at best and even atheism at its worst. Prayerlessness suggests a belief that the material things we see and feel are the only things that are real. Prayerlessness says I can tackle the task before me with the resources I have at my disposal in this material world—my money, buildings, intelligence, physical strength, intellectual capacity.

When we do not pray, this is the hidden assumption driving our life and ministry. And it is so naïve, is it not? We easily default to such worldly thinking, but this is dangerous. We are engaged in a spiritual task, a spiritual battle, and we have a spiritual Enemy.

We can be naïve and even arrogant about this. But how striking to see the way the apostle Paul approached his ministry endeavours. He knew he needed help. He knew the work was beyond him. As such, he was proactive in repeatedly asking for prayer. Look again at Ephesians 6. We are in a spiritual battle. Pray at all times in the Spirit for all the saints. And then Paul requests prayer, "also for me, that words may be given me in opening my mouth boldly to proclaim the mystery of the gospel" (v. 19).

I need help. I am aware of it. I cannot do this on my own. This is beyond me.

Likewise, Paul asks the Colossian Christians, "Continue steadfastly in prayer, being watchful in it with thanksgiving. At the same time, pray also for us, that God may open to us a door for the word, to declare the mystery of Christ, on account of which I am in prison—that I may make it clear, which is how I ought to speak" (Col. 4:2–4).

We must pray for one another in the work of ministry, and for our leaders, pastors, and elders. How we each need prayer. Let us pray for one another in our congregations. With our Lord's enabling, let us be a praying family, faithfully proclaiming Christ and loving the people God sends to us. Let us pray for spiritual fruit and protection from the devil's schemes.

In 2 Corinthians 12 Paul recounts how the Lord taught him again of his weakness when the joy and wonder of his spiritual experience threatened to make him proud. He confesses:

So to keep me from becoming conceited because of the surpassing greatness of the revelations, a thorn was given me in the flesh, a messenger of Satan to harass me, to keep me from becoming conceited. Three times I pleaded with the Lord about this, that it should leave me. But he said to me, "My grace is sufficient for you, for my power is made perfect in weakness." Therefore I will boast all the more gladly of my weaknesses, so that the power of Christ may rest upon me. (vv. 7–9)

We should be a little nervous—probably very nervous—if ever we feel strong, successful, powerful, or triumphant in our ministry. If we are part of a larger church or influential ministry that has known blessing, we should be cautious.

Being conscious of our weakness is right and healthy. We are weak; that is the truth of it, of course. We are made of frail flesh, each one of us. We are less holy than we ought to be and more sinful than we care to admit. We are not nearly as wise as we think we are. Our ministry has flaws. We get things wrong. We miss things. We overlook people. We ignore opportunities. We wish we could do better. *We are weak—that is the bottom line.*

But praise the Lord that He shows us our weakness and makes us conscious of our weakness because weakness drives us to our knees, and when we fall on our knees before Him, His power is released. When we are weak—*precisely when we are weak*—we discover how strong He is.

I hope we know how weak we are. I hope our frailty drives us to pray, and I hope we will never depart from the place of dependency where spiritual power is released. Let us pray because the work is beyond us. Let us pray because the Father enables those who look to Him for strength.

Four, we are to be a people of prayer because of the Father's willingness. In prayer we are not crying out to a closed heaven. We are not marching on Parliament Hill or Capitol Hill, appealing in vain to leaders who can ignore us or even despise our pleas. We are not seeking to twist the arm of a resistant leader or an unyielding tyrant.

No, we are coming to our Father. Our Father loves us and is more committed to our good than we are. Our Father knows what is best. He delights in our approach, in hearing our prayers, in answering them in accordance with His will. We come to a willing Father.

In 2 Chronicles 7, when the new temple was being dedicated, the Lord affirmed to King Solomon His willingness to hear the prayers of His people and to respond to them. Consider this lovely moment:

Then the LORD appeared to Solomon in the night and said to him: "I have heard your prayer and have chosen this place for myself as a house of sacrifice. When I shut up the heavens so that there is no rain, or command the locust to devour the land, or send pestilence among my people, if my people who are called by my name humble themselves, and pray and seek my face and turn from their wicked ways, then I will hear from heaven and will forgive their sin and heal their land. Now my eyes will be open and my ears attentive to the prayer that is made in this place." (vv. 12–15)

Of course, we do not need the temple building as a place of prayer anymore. Jesus, our great High Priest, takes us to the heavenly sanctuary. But the heart of God is unchanged. He is ready, willing, and eager to hear and answer our prayer.

There is no lack of willingness or ability on the part of God to answer our prayers. He is ready to do more than we ask, more than we can even contemplate; but we so often fail to ask. He is the One, as Paul says in Ephesians 3:20, "who is able to do far more abundantly than all that we ask or think, according to the power at work within us."

Remember what Jesus said of the Father in Matthew 7:7–11:

> "Ask, and it will be given to you; seek, and you will find; knock, and it will be opened to you. For everyone who asks receives, and the one who seeks finds, and to the one who knocks it will be opened. Or which one of you, if his son asks him for bread, will give him a stone? Or if he asks for a fish, will give him a serpent? If you then, who are evil, know how to give good gifts to your children, how much more will your Father who is in heaven give good things to those who ask him!"

I wonder what we may not have because we do not ask.

I was struck to read the results of a Barna survey reporting that 75 percent of teenagers in the United States say they want to know more about Jesus.[7] I almost fell out of my chair when I saw that. *Three-quarters of teenagers want to know more about Jesus.*

We are so conditioned to be pessimistic. "People do not want to know about Jesus; there will not be a response. Everything is going downhill, and on it goes." But hold on! There is a readiness among many of the younger generation—*a readiness and*

---

7. "Over Half of Gen Z Teens Feel Motivated to Learn More about Jesus," Barna, February 1, 2023, https://www.barna.com/research/teens-and-jesus.

even an eagerness—to hear. Why are we not on our knees praying for a powerful work of the Spirit for thousands upon thousands and millions upon millions of young people to find life in Christ?

I love this hymn of John Newton's. Listen to his words:

> *Come, my soul, thy suit prepare:*
> *Jesus loves to answer prayer;*
> *He Himself has bid thee pray,*
> *Therefore will not say thee nay.*
>
> *Thou art coming to a King,*
> *Large petitions with thee bring;*
> *For His grace and power are such,*
> *None can ever ask too much.*[8]

Do we hear the Father's instruction and invitation?

Do we see the extraordinary way in which He has opened the door to us in the gospel and through the priestly work of our Savior? Do we see this great privilege? Do we recognize the spiritual nature of our task and the challenges before us?

Do we acknowledge our weakness and long that, through dependency, our weakness might become strength in Him through His enabling power? Do we believe He is willing and

---

8. John Newton, "Encouragement to Pray," 1779, public domain.

able—*so willing and so able*—to hear and answer the prayers of His children as we come in accordance with His will?

We will grow in health, vitality, maturity, and effectiveness the more we are given to prayer.

Let us be a praying people, a praying family, that the Lord might work powerfully through us for His glory.

8

. . . .

Gathered to Care

WHY DO WE GATHER AS THE PEOPLE OF GOD IN THE
fellowship of the local church, and what good purpose does
God have for us in this? We have all seen or heard of exam-
ples of unhealthy churches. We know stories of hurt and disappointment. Sadly, churches can easily lose their way and
become unhealthy, dysfunctional, and distorted in their culture
or ministry.

Of course, one way for a church to go quickly off the rails
is to abandon core biblical doctrines and loosen its grip on
essential theological convictions. If a church begins compro-
mising on core ethical matters or bending on its doctrine of

Scripture, the Trinity, or the atonement, the drift and distortion can quickly become evident.

This, however, is not the only way things can go awry. After all, it is hardly the case that every theologically sound church is healthy. We could have a great statement of faith but be an unhealthy fellowship.

So, what does a healthy church culture look like according to Scripture? What will it mean for me to play my part in cultivating that culture, and how can I invest in this community in a way that is purposeful and biblical? Likewise, how might a theologically sound church fail to be a healthy church?

I believe one key way a fellowship may fail is by neglecting to care for one another as family. A church may be theologically solid, but if it is relationally weak, it falls short of what it means to be the people of God. We can have sound doctrine and dynamic exposition, but according to Scripture, that is not enough.

The Church Is a Family

The Bible makes clear that, as a people belonging to Jesus Christ, we are called into the family of God and called to treat one another as family.

Notice Jesus's words in Matthew 12:

> While he [Jesus] was still speaking to the people, behold, his mother and his brothers stood outside, asking to speak to him. But he replied to the man who told him, "Who is my mother, and who are my brothers?" And stretching out his hand toward his disciples, he said, "Here are my mother and my brothers! For whoever does the will of my Father in heaven is my brother and sister and mother." (vv. 46–50)

The message comes, *Jesus, your family is here.* He replies by asking who His family is. Then, He answers His own question: my family is anyone who knows the Lord in such a way that he or she does the Lord's will. They are His family.

When a person becomes a follower of Jesus, one of the things that happens right away is a radical reordering of relationships. When you and I come to Jesus Christ and place our trust in Him, God establishes in our lives a new relational order. Things change, and they change for good. The most fundamental change is that God welcomes us into His family.

Before coming to Christ, we were enemies of God and separated from Him because of our sin. We were divided from those around us. We were divided by religious barriers, like the barrier between Jew and Gentile. We were divided by race, tribe, language, and geography. We were divided by history and hostility, by class and by culture, and by so much more.

But in making us His own, God makes us part of His family. We become His sons and daughters. We are adopted in Christ. First John 3:1 says, "See what kind of love the Father has given to us, that we should be called children of God; and so we are."

What a marvelous miracle of grace. We were once His enemies, but God has not only made us His friends but, even more, His own children adopted in grace.

So Jesus takes the opportunity in Matthew 12 to drive home this point. Those who listen to His words, who are eager to follow and obey, are the family of God. They are His mother and sisters and brothers. They are dear to Him and tied to Him in meaningful relationship. And the same is true for us. If we know Jesus by faith, we are part of the family.

Now, we might say, "Well, that sounds lovely. It is a nice sentiment, but does it really add up to anything?" I remember buying a car once, and the people at the dealership were friendly and helpful. I remember the salesman saying to me when I bought the car, "Now, you're part of the family." It struck me as nice but perhaps a little strange. Over time, I came to see that this sentiment was part of the dealership's marketing strategy, appearing in their email campaigns and elsewhere. "We're family" was their slogan.

And I have to say, the cynical part of my mind did not respond well to that bit of marketing. I began to think: *Okay, where is my birthday card? Presents, maybe? We would like to drop*

the kids off for babysitting on Friday night—you okay with that?
We are going away for a few days. Would you mind stopping by and
mowing the lawn for us? I mean, we are family, after all.

If we are family, surely that means more than simply being willing to service my car from time to time (at considerable expense) and emailing me about once a month, suggesting I buy another car from you. Being family is a different thing altogether.

We easily grow cynical with such marketing. In the same way, we could hear this idea that Christians are family, and the church is a family, and grow cynical. *It sounds nice, but it does not mean much.*

So, what does it mean that we are part of the family of God? What does it mean that the church is a family first and foremost?

The Church Is a Family that Cares

Being part of the family of God means we care for one another, and we care for one another well. We are not just a family—*we are a caring family.*

Sadly, you know families that do not care for or take an interest in one another's lives. You see dysfunctional families, neglected children, estranged relatives, and forgotten or cast-aside members. But that is not how a family should be. And as believers, as a church, if we are a healthy family, we are a family that cares well for one another.

For each of us, this is a real moment when our profession of faith in Christ must have a practical outworking if it is genuine. This is a moment of challenge and opportunity, but it is a moment we cannot escape.

Even so, how easily we can sneak in the back row a little late on Sunday morning, rush out the door early, or come simply for the preaching of the Word and for corporate worship. We may take part in those things and even enjoy them, but have little involvement in others' lives. We do not know them, and we are not known by them.

Of course, in recent years, with the impact of the pandemic and the growth of live streaming of services (which may have a useful, ongoing place), there has been a radical shift in the nature of church participation. Many people now access church services and teaching remotely and online. For the shut-in or the person who lives in a remote place or the person going through temporary hardship, digital media can be a great blessing.

But here is the danger: the one who streams the service only or comes in late, leaves early, and speaks to no one is essentially a consumer of ministry. This person is an observer and a recipient to an extent, but is not really part of the family.

To stay in that position over time is a recipe for spiritual dysfunction—and not only for personal dysfunction but also for corporate, family dysfunction. This consumer mindset brings dysfunction to the whole church.

Conversely, a healthy church is a gathering of members who care one for another. Within a wider overview of the marks of true Christian living set forth in Romans 12, the apostle Paul gives us a window into the nature of Christian community and care within the family. Consider what he writes in Romans 12:9–16:

> Let love be genuine. Abhor what is evil; hold fast to what is good. Love one another with brotherly affection. Outdo one another in showing honor. Do not be slothful in zeal, be fervent in spirit, serve the Lord. Rejoice in hope, be patient in tribulation, be constant in prayer. Contribute to the needs of the saints and seek to show hospitality.
>
> Bless those who persecute you; bless and do not curse them. Rejoice with those who rejoice, weep with those who weep. Live in harmony with one another. Do not be haughty, but associate with the lowly. Never be wise in your own sight.

Now, we will not parse and unpack everything Paul says here, but notice *the scope of care* we are to have one for another in Christian community.

We are to have a genuine love for one another (v. 9). This love is not merely superficial greetings in the corridor, but family love. This love cherishes and is concerned for the well-being of the other. It causes us to be willing to bear cost for one another and to inconvenience ourselves for one another. We are to love one another, says verse 10, with a brotherly and sisterly affection. Furthermore, that affection results in us even competing with one another to show honor to others within the family—to show them that we treasure and prize them and truly hold them in our heart.

There are not too many occasions in Scripture where we are encouraged to compete with one another (I cannot think of any others currently), but here is one. We are to seek to outdo one another in showing honor to one another. We are to strive to be good at that—to be the very best at that—by the Spirit's help.

Now, how is this love for one another going to be expressed? How is this prizing and honoring one another going to be shown? Paul points us in two directions here in the text. He shows us that we are to care for one another *on a practical level* and *on an emotional and spiritual level.* That is, we care *with our hands*, and we care *with our heart.*

Notice the practical element in verse 13: "Contribute to the needs of the saints and seek to show hospitality."

If we have a true brotherly affection for one another and seek to honor one another, we will respond to their needs. If we hear of brothers and sisters who have lost their jobs, cannot feed their families, are about to lose their home, are facing illness, or whatever their need, here is what the family does: the family gets together and does what it can to help meet that need. We do not do this blindly and thoughtlessly or throw money at someone who is being irresponsible; rather, if a saint is in need, the family is there.

Part of meeting those practical needs involves hospitality; part of showing practical care for the family involves using our own homes. If a family in the church has a flood or a fire and they need somewhere to stay, they should have a long list of invitations by nightfall. If a new believer joins the fellowship after moving from out of town, not knowing anyone, it should not be long before she has an invitation to a home for a meal to be with family.

Many churches will have in place some form of benevolence ministry. I am grateful that our church has long had in place such a ministry. Church members regularly donate to a fund. When unemployment strikes, illness comes, or the paycheck just does not stretch to cover the grocery bill one month, someone can confidentially share the need and receive support.

Over the course of the year, many needs are met, many families helped, and many brothers and sisters know they are loved and cared for by the family. What a beautiful ministry of the body of Christ.

Scripture says that being part of the family means caring in practical terms. Caring involves our hands. Caring also involves our heart. Alongside caring for one another practically is a call for us to care for one another spiritually and emotionally. Notice Romans 12:15: "Rejoice with those who rejoice, weep with those who weep."

The world around us is full of joy and sorrow. Our news and social media feeds give us a constant stream of reports and images of both. We hear and see news of people succeeding in their work, delighting in relationships, marriage, children, and milestones. If you are on Facebook or Instagram, you see the joy in a steady flow of images and updates. But at some point, your capacity to give emotion to share in all that joy with strangers is too much. It floods over you.

And similarly with grief and sorrow. Our news feed and social media accounts tell us so much. I recently saw on my feed a post from someone I do not know at all just saying, *Please pray for me; my family is in desperate need*. You see posts from people you have never met who share about losing a loved one. The other night, a post came up on a neighborhood feed telling news of a terrible road accident near our home. We felt so much grief and stopped to take time to pray for the families and the injured. Or you may see a news report about a violent attack or conflict on the other side of the world. You feel the pang of grief over it and stop to pray. Even so, I think we understand feeling overwhelmed and the need to step back from the torrent of such reports in this information age.

Now, we cannot carry all the individual and collective griefs of the whole community on our heart, and we certainly cannot carry the suffering of the whole world. But here is what we can do and must do: we must open our heart in love to those whom God puts before us, and especially those in our church family, and "rejoice with those who rejoice, [and] weep with those who weep" (v. 15).

Opening our heart involves an emotional investment and an intentionality. It is one of the great marks of the church of Jesus Christ. The world may not care about the joy you are experiencing in a marriage, in the birth of a child, in the success at school after years of struggling, in landing that job, or in getting the all-clear from the doctor. The cold and uncaring world may not bat an eyelid. But we should come into the fellowship, step into the door of the church, and find brothers and sisters whose hearts are open and soft toward us in such a way that they enter into our joy. They make our cause their own in their heart so that a joy for us is a joy for them as well.

Likewise, you may have lost a loved one—a parent, spouse, or child—and feel as though the walls have started crowding around you. Your life seems like it is falling apart. Your heart is broken; the loss is overwhelming. All seems darkness for a time. Then, you go out into the wide community, and people do not know your sorrow, or if they know, they seem to not care. You observe that for everyone else, life is carrying on and others do not see your pain, and that makes it all the worse to bear.

But the family of God is different. The church is unlike the world in this. We step into church and find a spiritual family who loves us. Our brothers and sisters are grieved because we are grieved. Our loss is meaningful to them because *we* are meaningful to them. We find people who will grieve with us, weep with us, and walk alongside us. This does not take the pain away, but, oh, it changes the experience. Their love softens the harshness of our loss and somehow makes it more bearable. We feel loved. We feel known and cared for, and it is one of the greatest gifts we can receive in times of mourning.

Friend, you cannot be part of that if you only watch church online or come late and leave early and avoid talking to anyone. You cannot be part of the family in that way.

We all need to be actively involved in recognizing the needs of others. You might think your church has a church staff and pastors who do this ministry. Just keep your head down and avoid eye contact with the grieving or rejoicing because you are busy and do not have time. No, whatever the size of the fellowship, the staff and leaders can never enter into every joy and every sorrow and be all the family needs them to be. No, this is for *all* of us. This is a shared privilege and responsibility. Every member of the family must play his or her part.

How precious when brothers and sisters come alongside, often quietly, to share in meeting a need and being the family of God. Alongside sharing one another's joys and sorrows, we carry a broader responsibility of care for one another in terms of our *spiritual health*. We are to seek how we can encourage one another in our walk with the Lord. As we have seen already, encouragement is at the heart of why we gather together on Sundays. We want to see one another and take every opportunity to encourage one another.

The well-known exhortation of Hebrews 10:24–25 emphasizes this: "And let us consider how to stir up one another to love and good works, not neglecting to meet together, as is the habit of some, but encouraging one another, and all the more as you see the Day drawing near."

This passage prompts us to come to church with a purposeful mindset for action, thinking: *Who can I encourage today in their walk with Jesus? Who can I stir up with a kind word to love and good works?* That may not be our natural mindset as we make our way to church on a Sunday morning, but it is a transformative mindset if we grab hold of it.

Within the family, we want to be looking out particularly for those who are struggling and stumbling. If you attend a family gathering and you perceive someone is struggling, you do not want to ignore it. You want to help if you can. Each member of the family is valuable and precious. You love them.

Consider especially Paul's exhortation in Galatians 6:1–2: "Brothers, if anyone is caught in any transgression, you who are spiritual should restore him in a spirit of gentleness. Keep watch on yourself, lest you too be tempted. Bear one another's burdens, and so fulfill the law of Christ."

Now, we all like our personal space; we value our independence and privacy. In Western society, we are geared to keep to ourselves and not meddle in other people's lives. Equally, we expect others not to meddle in ours.

So we may feel somewhat vexed that Scripture exhorts us to take an interest in other people's lives to this degree. If a brother or sister stumbles and falls into sin that brings messy consequences, rather than stay as far out of it as we can, those who are spiritually mature should walk toward that person and not away. They should take prayerful interest in their restoration. They should seek to get others back on their feet and walking with the Lord again.

Imagine you are driving in a remote place, and you come upon a car that has broken down on the side of the road or has been in an accident. Do you simply drive on by, or do you stop and help? Do you stay comfortable in your own car with music playing, windows up, and sunglasses on, or do you allow your plans to be disrupted, your time to be taken, your comfort compromised perhaps, and stop and see what you can do?

On a spiritual level, Paul is saying that within the family we do not leave people by the roadside. We do not just drive on by. No, we take an active interest in their spiritual well-being. We exercise care for them and help them get back on their way.

Moreover, we do it cautiously and carefully, just as we would be cautious in stopping by the side of the road. *Can I do this safely? Maybe, maybe not.* We need to be careful if we step in to help in a situation of sin that we are not tempted too (v. 1). Thus, in some situations we must pray and leave it to another who has more maturity or experience. But we do not simply ignore the need. We show love and exercise care.

Beyond walking with someone who has stumbled in sin, Paul generalizes this spiritual care more broadly in verse 2: "Bear one another's burdens, and so fulfill the law of Christ."

We do not carry alone the challenges of discipleship, the heaviness of life, the obstacles to growth, and the discouragements in our walk with the Lord. No, we are part of a family. We seek to be known and to involve ourselves in others' lives so that we are positioned and available to bear their burdens.

I may be discouraged and disheartened. Perhaps I am finding prayer hard and do not feel I am growing as I should. I notice gaps in my understanding of the Word; I do not know how to make sense of suffering and God's goodness in it. Or my personal evangelism is going nowhere. And you are in a position as my brother or sister in Christ to come alongside, to pray, to be an encouragement, and to bear that burden with me.

How do we do this? How do we become more and more a church family that really loves one another and cares for one another?

Well, it starts by being present in person regularly. It involves clearing the calendar, making church a priority, and showing up no matter how tired you are or what has happened that week. It starts by giving time on Sundays, before and after the service, to talk to people and get to know the family. Caring relationships develop when you become involved in a small group with people whom you can walk alongside more consistently. Similarly, when you are standing shoulder to shoulder with others in the trenches doing the work of ministry, relationships grow. You know others' concerns, and you are ready to respond and be there when the joys and sorrows come.

As the people of God, as the church of Jesus Christ, we are a family. More than that, we are called to be a *caring* family—a family that truly cares for one another practically, relationally, and spiritually.

The Church Is a Family that Cares for the Outsider

Many have debated in recent years the role of the church in meeting practical needs in the community and engaging in acts of mercy. Whether to extend care beyond the church family can be a fraught question that is difficult to navigate.

Clearly from Scripture, the primary mission of the church is not to alleviate poverty or to engage in social work. Our mission is to make disciples of Jesus Christ through proclaiming His Word. We have in that sense an eternal mandate and must not be distracted by focusing on other good works that could take us away from gospel proclamation.

So the church of Jesus Christ is not a social agency. We must be clear about that. Nevertheless, according to Scripture, we do have a special responsibility to care for the practical needs of the saints as family. Does any of that practical care spill out beyond the church walls?

Interestingly, in Galatians 6, Paul indicates that our concern in the well-being and care for others does extend beyond the church family, even if our clear priority is the people of God. Notice verses 9 and 10: "And let us not grow weary of doing good, for in due season we will reap, if we do not give up. So then, as we have opportunity, let us do good to everyone, and especially to those who are of the household of faith."

Paul observes, "As we have opportunity." We do not look to manufacture and multiply opportunities because there is no end of practical need in the world. We cannot meet every need. However, as opportunity presents itself—as people come to us with needs or we see immediate needs on our doorstep in the community—let us do good to everyone. If a disaster occurs on our doorstep and people are in urgent need with no water or electricity, let us see how we can help and do good to them. Or if a mother comes and knocks on the church door and asks for help feeding her children, we do not shut the door. No, that is an opportunity to do good in the name of Jesus. We take that opportunity and cherish the opportunities to do good to those whom the Lord sends to us.

But the priority is, of course, the family of faith. We have a first-order responsibility to the people of God as family. We have an obligation to our brothers and sisters, but we love the wider opportunities God gives us.

And when we do so, we find that the Lord so often uses those practical opportunities to further our gospel mission. In fact, when someone in need receives from the people of God a gift of kindness like a grocery card to feed the household that week, or when a team of believers comes to a home after a storm and helps patch the roof or remove a fallen tree that is leaning against the house, so often, a door opens to explain why we would ever do that. The Lord uses practical opportunities frequently to open gospel opportunities.

The church is a family. The gathering of God's people is a family that cares and loves because we have first been loved. Are you part of the family? Have you entered in by faith in Jesus? And if you have, are you contributing to family life by caring practically and spiritually for the brothers and sisters God has given you?

9

. . . .

Gathered to Grow

ANGLICAN ARCHBISHOP WILLIAM TEMPLE FAMOUSLY
observed that the church of Jesus Christ stands apart in that
it is perhaps the only organization in the world that exists for
the benefit of those who are not its members. Few other organizations have such a central concern for those who do not yet
belong to it.

Temple may have overstated the point because the church's
own members do indeed benefit from being part of the church.
Nevertheless, his observation is not void of insight. The church
of Jesus Christ exists in a profound sense for the benefit of
those who are not yet part of it and who do not yet know the
Lord by faith.

It is lovely to see a growing family. When children and grandchildren are born or a family grows through adoption, we delight in this beautiful gift. It is lovely to see a community growing and a nation growing. Growth means life and vitality. A nation with a stagnant or declining population is in crisis with significant trouble on the horizon.

Growth in the church is also beautiful, healthy, and vital.

On the global scale, the church of Jesus Christ is huge and growing. About 2.6 billion people profess faith in Christ, which is nearly a third of the world's population. Even more, that number is growing by about 1.2 percent a year.[9] If we single out the evangelicals and Pentecostals, that growth rate is markedly higher. Such figures may be difficult to analyze, but however you calculate the numbers, the global church is huge, and it is growing.

And for the church, the family of God, growth matters in a unique way. We care about growth because it is a matter of life and death. When new people are added to the family of God by faith in Jesus Christ, it means they have been snatched from death and won for life. They have gone from being enemies of God to being His friends. They have been given hope and a future.

Individual congregations, of course, go through seasons of growth and decline for many reasons, some of which involve

---

9. https://www.gordonconwell.edu/wp-content/uploads/sites/13/2023/01/Status-of-Global-Christianity-2023.pdf, accessed June 12, 2024.

broader demographics in the community. But the global church of Jesus Christ, the family of which we are a part, *must be a growing family*. Growth is vitally important, and we long to see new people come to faith and join our local expression of the church. We love to witness gospel growth locally; we love to see new life in our midst. The family of God is a growing family and must be a growing family.

The first picture we are given of the post-Pentecost church is of a growing gathering of people who resembles an infant thriving in new life. Look at Acts 2:42–47 and the church in its earliest days:

> And they devoted themselves to the apostles' teaching and the fellowship, to the breaking of bread and the prayers. And awe came upon every soul, and many wonders and signs were being done through the apostles. And all who believed were together and had all things in common. And they were selling their possessions and belongings and distributing the proceeds to all, as any had need. And day by day, attending the temple together and breaking bread in their homes, they received their food with glad and generous hearts, praising God and having favor with all the people. And the

Lord added to their number day by day those
who were being saved.

This picture is healthy and heartening; it resonates with our
hearts as we imagine the scene. We know God's family must
grow, and we long for it to grow. We long to see the Lord add-
ing to our number day by day those who are being saved.

We long for that, but how does it happen? Growth occurs
in many ways and often organically. But as we look to the Bible,
several factors drive the growth of the church.

*First and foremost, the family grows through proclama-
tion.* Proclamation is at the heart of everything, according to
Scripture.

Consider 1 Peter 1:22–25:

> Having purified your souls by your obedience
> to the truth for a sincere brotherly love, love
> one another earnestly from a pure heart, since
> you have been born again, not of perishable
> seed but imperishable, through the living and
> abiding word of God; for
>
> "All flesh is like grass
>   and all its glory like the flower of grass.
> The grass withers,
>   and the flower falls,
> but the word of the Lord remains forever."

And this word is the good news that was
preached to you.

Peter makes a blanket statement here that applies to those
early Christians he is addressing and those who would read his
letter through the ages. He reminds us that we have come to
new birth "through the living and abiding word of God" (v. 23).
Additionally, "this word is the good news that was preached to
you" (v. 25).

No believer has ever come to faith except through the living
and life-giving Word of God. The normal means by which this
happens is through the preaching (that is, the public proclamation) of the Word.

Generally, the public preaching of the Word of God will be
at the heart of a story of conversion. That is true much of the
time, even most of the time. But even if a person receives the
Word somewhere else and somehow else, the Word is still the
means and mechanism of salvation. And that is the case because
of the nature of the gospel. Remember that *gospel* means "good
news." It is a message we must hear and receive.

Just to underline the point, let us look at another passage,
Romans 10, that makes the same emphasis. Here, Paul is setting out the central importance of preaching for the gospel of
salvation to go out.

In Romans 10:13 he reminds us of the promise of God that
"everyone who calls on the name of the Lord will be saved." He

then asks a series of penetrating questions that take us inescapably to the conclusion that preaching is essential. Notice the flow of logic in verses 14–17:

> How then will they call on him in whom they have not believed? And how are they to believe in him of whom they have never heard? And how are they to hear without someone preaching? And how are they to preach unless they are sent? As it is written, "How beautiful are the feet of those who preach the good news!" But they have not all obeyed the gospel. For Isaiah says, "Lord, who has believed what he has heard from us?" So faith comes from hearing, and hearing through the word of Christ.

We need to call on the name of the Lord to be saved. Jesus has come as our Savior. He died in our place to pay the price of our sin and to purchase our forgiveness. We access that salvation through repentance and faith, through calling on the name of the Lord Jesus. Yet we cannot do that if we do not know of Him and if we have not heard the message of salvation, the good news. And so it must be preached.

An oft-quoted aphorism frequently attributed (perhaps in error) to Francis of Assisi regularly does the rounds in Christian circles. You have probably heard it: "Preach the gospel always; use words if necessary."

Of course, the idea that our lives should be a witness is important, and we are going to address that. But it is nonsensical to suggest that we can preach the gospel without speaking. Preaching is inherently verbal. The gospel is a message that must be articulated and expressed verbally. No one will ever be saved simply because you and I are nice people, to the extent that we are nice. Yes, it is nice to be nice, but that will not save anyone.

No, dead people are born again through the living and enduring Word of God—through the preached word. Everyone who calls on the name of the Lord will be saved, but they need to hear His name and receive His message. And His message needs to be preached.

The emphasis Paul places on *hearing* that preached word in Romans 10 is interesting. Notice again verse 17: "So faith comes from hearing, and hearing through the word of Christ."

We receive the gospel just by hearing it. We do not go and do things to receive Christ. Our salvation is a gift of pure grace, received by faith. And so it fits perfectly that this message is something we hear. It comes to us as listeners and recipients.

That is why the proclamation of the gospel is at the heart of how we grow as a family. The preaching of the Word is the engine of growth and why many churches make its exposition the main event on a Sunday morning. It is why we are so eager to invite our unbelieving friends and family to come to hear the message. It is why at special times in the year, such as Christmas and Easter, our great burden is to invite people to hear the message of salvation and sit under the preaching of the Word. We believe in the power of the Word and the preaching of it.

This conviction is what drives Word-centered churches to put the Word of God at the heart of every ministry and activity. In the church I serve, you will be hard-pressed to come to any event and not hear the Word of God in some form. That is intentional; it is convictional. We believe God brings dead people to spiritual life through His living and abiding Word.

How does the church grow, and how does the family grow? How do people come to new life? Growth occurs through the proclamation of the Word of God.

Two, the family grows through parenting; namely, godly parenting. This might sound a little surprising as a teaching point on this theme, but godly parenting is vitally important for church growth.

In fact, you may be a follower of Christ because your parents or grandparents taught you the Word of God and told you the gospel. Of course, you may have come to faith from a background in atheism or another religion. But many of us come to faith in Christ through a believing family and godly home. Believing parents have a profound influence on their children.

A godly home was a key part of Timothy's testimony in the early church, which Paul emphasizes in his letter to him in 2 Timothy 1:5: "I am reminded of your sincere faith, a faith that dwelt first in your grandmother Lois and your mother Eunice and now, I am sure, dwells in you as well." Paul refers to the influence of family on Timothy's spiritual life again in chapter 3 when he admonishes him: "But as for you, continue in what you have learned and have firmly believed, knowing from whom you learned it and how from childhood you have been acquainted with the sacred writings, which are able to make you wise for salvation through faith in Christ Jesus" (vv. 14–15).

Paul saw that Timothy was the product of a godly family—at least he had the clear benefit of the influence of a godly mother and grandmother. Now here is Timothy, all grown up, and himself so significant and influential in the work of the kingdom. Timothy's story is noteworthy, but it is not the exception. The Bible leads us to expect that parents and grandparents are going to play an outsized role in the spiritual development of their children.

Proverbs 22:6 says, "Train up a child in the way he should go; even when he is old he will not depart from it."

In Deuteronomy 6:4–9, the Lord's people receive this charge:

> "Hear, O Israel: The LORD our God, the LORD
> is one. You shall love the LORD your God with

all your heart and with all your soul and with all your might. And these words that I command you today shall be on your heart. You shall teach them diligently to your children, and shall talk of them when you sit in your house, and when you walk by the way, and when you lie down, and when you rise. You shall bind them as a sign on your hand, and they shall be as frontlets between your eyes. You shall write them on the doorposts of your house and on your gates."

If the Lord has entrusted children to you, here is your job description and charge from the Lord: Teach your children the Word of God. Point them to the Savior. Lead them to the cross, and guide them in the way they should go. Then, pray that the Lord might be at work in the hearts of your children, drawing them to Himself, giving them faith, keeping them in His goodness. As believing parents do this and are supported by believing grandparents, too, the family of God grows naturally.

In the work of the kingdom, we need to remember our role as parents. We must keep in mind the fact that we are the primary evangelists for our children. We do not outsource that role and hope for the best or for the Sunday school teacher to take care of them for us. No, we need to make the most of the opportunities we have with our children at home to point them to Christ and to speak the Word of God into their lives. The window of opportunity is narrow; children grow up quickly. We have to be parents and grandparents who intentionally pray for them. We need to take seriously the gospel work that is done at home and seek to support the children's ministry in our local fellowship.

The family grows through parents who point their children to the Savior.

Three, the family grows through personal evangelism. Proverbs 6 commends to us the image of the ant as an effective worker. I am reminded of that image because we seem to have an unusual number of those workers visiting our home at the moment! Actually, the industrious ant working in tandem with his coworkers is a fitting metaphor as we consider our collective role in evangelism as a whole church.

We can easily think evangelism is for missionaries to do or the outreach director or the pastors. But the truth of the matter is that you have the contacts. You know the people. You are on the evangelistic front lines in your families, neighborhoods, schools, colleges, residences, workplaces, and sports team.

You have a vital role to play. Consider again the tiny ant. When you see ants in a colony, they are all active. You do not see two ants doing all the work and five hundred ants lying back on lounge chairs with a book and a cold drink. No, they are all engaged in the effort. They are all active.

Likewise, you and I need to be in this work together. Each of us will play our part in different ways but engage similarly. *In the first place, we must pray.* Specifically, I would encourage you to identify a few people in each season of life and pray regularly for opportunities with them and for their salvation.

Another thing we can do is invite. We can invite friends, family, and colleagues to key events at church where the gospel will be proclaimed.

I was at lunch with one of our missionaries one day, and he struck up a conversation with our server in the restaurant. He introduced me as the pastor of the church across the river, and she said to me, "Oh, I've been to your church. My neighbor invited me at Christmas."

And I thought, *Fantastic!* What a thrill to meet her and to follow up with my missionary friend on the work begun by this young woman's neighbor and my fellow church member. That is teamwork and the Lord's kindness encouraging us.

Beyond giving invitations to events, we need to speak of Christ ourselves. First Peter 3:15 exhorts us: "but in your hearts honor Christ the Lord as holy, always being prepared to make a defense to anyone who asks you for a reason for the hope that is in you; yet do it with gentleness and respect."

Added to all this, we need to be constantly ready. Let us be ready and "always prepared"—willing to speak of Christ rather than frightened or ashamed. Let us be ready with what we might say. Readiness prompts us to ask ourselves: Do I know how to explain the gospel in simple terms? Do I know how to explain to someone the reason for the hope I have? Do I know how to speak of what Jesus means to me and what He has done for me?

Let us be ready to share the gospel and know how to do that with gentleness and respect. As we each pray specifically, invite others, proclaim Christ, and ready ourselves to share the gospel, we witness the power of a coordinated God-honoring kingdom effort. My individual efforts may not seem like much, and your individual efforts might not seem like much, but the whole family working together and prayerfully engaging in making Christ known is powerful. The Lord can use that combined effort in remarkable ways to grow the family.

The family grows through personal evangelism.

Four, the family grows through our practical witness. I mentioned before the oft-quoted aphorism that we should "preach the gospel always; use words if necessary."

Well, words are necessary. No one will come to faith without us speaking. Nevertheless, the witness of our actions—the witness of our community life—does matter. It is significant. The collective witness of our community life either commends the gospel or detracts from the gospel. People will see the way we live, the way we interact with others, and how we treat them, and then find our lives compelling; or they will look on and choose to have nothing to do with us.

I think the compelling witness of the community was at the heart of the reason the church grew in Acts 2. Look again at the picture:

> And all who believed were together and had all things in common. And they were selling their possessions and belongings and distributing the proceeds to all, as any had need. And day by day, attending the temple together and breaking bread in their homes, they received their food with glad and generous hearts, praising God and having favor with all the people. And the Lord added to their number day by day those who were being saved. (vv. 44–47)

Now, that is a snapshot of a remarkable time. The Bible does not say we must abolish private property and sell everything we own. Even so, we see here in Acts 2 a community radically devoted to the Lord and to one another. We see a community marked by love for one another and thanksgiving. And this community gained favor with all the people. People looked on and saw that something remarkable was happening here. As they looked on, a steady stream came to faith: "The Lord added to their number day by day those who were being saved."

The Lord Jesus makes clear that He wants us to be distinctive as His people in a dark world and a decaying society. Using memorable imagery, He calls us to be "salt and light"; that is, to have a distinctive flavor—perhaps a preserving influence—and to be visibly different in a dark world.

Jesus says,

> "You are the salt of the earth, but if salt has lost its taste, how shall its saltiness be restored? It is no longer good for anything except to be thrown out and trampled under people's feet.
>
> "You are the light of the world. A city set on a hill cannot be hidden. Nor do a people light a lamp and put it under a basket, but on a stand, and it gives light to all in the house. In the same way, let your light shine before others, so that they may see your good works and give glory to your Father who is in heaven." (Matt. 5:13–16)

Jesus tells us His people are to be distinctive in the community and in the world. We are to have a distinctive flavor like salt; something about us ought to make an impression for good. Salt adds taste and stops decay, as does the church. We stand out as distinctive, and our influence in the community, nation, and world slows the rot and has a preserving effect on society.

Similarly, in the darkness we are light. We are a city on a hill—a visible place, an attractive place, a place of refuge. So the church is not meant to be hiding in the shadows. No, it is called to be visible, noticeable, distinctive, and attractive.

Why must we be visible? Notice the emphasis and the purpose: "Let your light shine before others, so that they may see your good works and give glory to your Father who is in heaven."

The purpose here is that others would look on, see something that stands out in an attractive way (in particular, good works), and make the connection between us and the God we serve. Seeing our good works, they will be moved to give Him glory. Of course, ultimately that will happen as they trust His Son and enter His kingdom themselves.

Now, as we discussed in the previous chapter, the church does not position itself to be a social agency. We do not attempt to meet every practical need in the community, to address every disaster, or to supply every need for shelter or food or clothing. We could not do that, of course. Whether we are a small or large congregation, we have limited resources, and we would quickly lose sight of the ministry of the Word if we tried to address every practical need. We would soon be overwhelmed, and the practicalities would squeeze out the proclamation. Plenty of well-intentioned ministries and missions have lost their gospel focus in that way before now, and we find cautionary tales in the history books and on the ministry landscape. And yet, when an urgent need comes to us and is presented before us, we must not close our ears and eyes to it. When the community calls on us to help during disaster, we must try to respond. When someone comes to our door and asks for practical assistance in a personal emergency, our door ought to be open, and we should be eager to help when and where we can.

Again, when the Lord gives opportunities to serve our community and we reach out with our hands and hearts, we will witness doors open for the gospel. As we seek to do good to all, God allows us to bear witness to Him. He allows us to be salt and light in a tangible way, and people who have not known the Lord return praise to Him. And, in the Lord's goodness, the family grows through our practical witness.

The family of God is a global and growing family. We want the family to grow because we want men, women, boys, and girls to know life in Christ and find hope in Him for time and eternity. We care about growth because growth is literally a matter of life and death. When new people join the family of God by faith in Jesus Christ, they have gone from being enemies of God to being His friends for eternity. They have been given hope and a future.

How does the gathering of God's people grow?

The family of God grows through the proclamation of the living and enduring Word of God, through godly parents who speak and model the gospel at home, through personal evangelism as we each prayerfully and boldly play our part, and through our collective witness. The family grows when the world sees in us something different, distinctive, and attractive, and the doors open to speak words of life.

God has called us together to something profoundly good—to a gathering shaped by grace that nourishes God's people in grace and extends His message of grace to a needy world.

May the Lord make us faithful witnesses in our local congregations around the world, and may He add to our number those who are being saved.

CONCLUSION

• • • • • • •

A Truly Good Design

THE CHRISTIAN LIFE IS LIVED IN THE CONTEXT OF THE local church. That is God's intention. That is the pattern set out for us in the Bible. Jesus came to save people who were scattered by sin and alienated from God and from one another. He came to gather us together in grace, as a family. The gathering of the local church pictures the gospel in a beautiful way and points us to the heavenly gathering of the saints, of which we are a part even now and which we will one day experience fully.

Some reading this book have stepped away from involvement in the church, or you have never become involved in the first place. Reasons for this will, no doubt, vary. For some, it might be a negative experience in the past; for others, it could be a lack of conviction of the importance of church; for others, the circumstances of life may have just gotten in the way.

My prayer is that this book will, first of all, have been an encouragement to you to find a church that teaches the Bible and lives out the gospel, and then I pray that you will commit, "nailing your colors to the mast." Let me caution you and temper your expectations: you will never find the perfect church. But there are so many churches out there where the love of Jesus is proclaimed from His Word and lived out among His people, why not make it your business to find such a church and to commit yourself to your brothers and sisters there?

For those of us who are already committed to a local church, my prayer is that this book will help us grow in godliness in our own participation and contribution to the life of the church—that we might be constructive and fruitful members of the body, serving one another well and honoring our Lord who purchased us at such great cost.

For groups or whole congregations who have read this book together, I trust that the Lord might use it to continue to shape your church to reflect more and more His good design, that your church may be a place where the gospel is heard and seen, experienced and enjoyed, all for His glory.